Modernist
Estates

Frances Lincoln Limited
74–77 White Lion Street
London N1 9PF
www.franceslincoln.com

Modernist Estates:
The buildings and the people who live in them today
Introduction by Douglas Murphy
Photography by Stefi Orazi unless otherwise credited
Design by Stefi Orazi Studio

First Frances Lincoln edition 2015

A catalogue record for this book is available
from the British Library.
ISBN 978-0-7112-3675-2

Printed and bound in China
1 2 3 4 5 6 7 8 9

Modernist Estates

The buildings and the people who live in them today

by Stefi Orazi

F

FRANCES LINCOLN LIMITED
PUBLISHERS

Cover

Design for Keeling House, Claredale Street Estate,
Bethnal Green, London. Section showing residents on
the twelfth- and thirteenth-floor balcony areas.

Image credits

Cover: © Lasdun Archive / RIBA Library Drawings & Archives Collections
pp. 12, 62, 90, 124, 174: © RIBA Library Photographs Collection
pp. 20, 36, 98: © London Metropolitan Archives, City of London
pp. 28, 54, 108: © John Maltby / RIBA Library Photographs Collection
pp. 44, 72, 116: © Architectural Press Archive / RIBA Library Photographs Collection
p. 57: © David McKendrick
p. 82: © David Borland / RIBA Library Photographs Collection
p. 132: © Tony Ray-Jones / RIBA Library Photographs Collection
p. 140: Photography by Eric De Mare © English Heritage
pp. 148, 158, 166: © Martin Charles / RIBA Library Photographs Collection
p. 168: © Jess Bonham
pp. 169–173: © Chrissie MacDonald / Andrew Rae

Acknowledgements

The author would like to extend her special thanks to
all the residents who contributed to the realisation
of this book and to the following individuals in their
invaluable support and guidance:

Nicki Davis
Georgia Dehn
David McKendrick
Mem Morrison
Kate Rogers

Author biographies

Douglas Murphy is an architecture critic living and working in London.
He is architecture correspondent at *Icon* magazine, and writes for a
variety of publications including the *Guardian*, *Architectural Review*,
New Humanist and others. He is the author of *The Architecture of Failure*
and the forthcoming *Last Futures*.

Stefi Orazi runs a small design studio in London, working with clients
such as the Barbican Art Gallery, Tate, Design Museum and *Wallpaper**.
She is renowned for her graphic illustrations and prints of modernist
architectural landmarks, and is the author of the blog modernistestates.com.

Contents

07 Foreword
08 Introduction by Douglas Murphy

13 Isokon
21 Pullman Court
29 Golden Lane Estate
37 Keeling House
45 The Hall
55 Dulwich Wood Park Estate
63 Manygate Lane
73 Park Hill
83 Sivill House
91 Balfron Tower
99 Perronet House
109 Barbican Estate
117 Brunswick
125 Byker
133 Lillington Gardens
141 Christchurch Estate
149 Dunboyne Road Estate
159 Alexandra and Ainsworth Estate
167 Whittington Estate
175 London Borough of Lambeth
183 Greenwich Millennium Village

Foreword

Apart from three years in University digs, I have always lived in a purpose-built flat. I grew up in an architecturally unremarkable council estate in Sussex, but the wibbly-wobbly layout of the Victorian houses of my more affluent school friends never really appealed.

My mother was born in a prefab just after the Second World War, and my ninety-four-year-old grandmother lives in an ordinary council house to this day. So I guess straight lines, built-in cupboards and functional modest spaces are in my blood and appeal to my rational graphic designer's brain. But it wasn't until I had the fortune of renting a room in a fantastic flat in the Barbican that modernist architecture became more of an obsession. It goes beyond the aesthetic, although I go weak at the knees at the sight of a beautifully detailed sliding door or a cantilevered staircase. It was the ideals and the optimism of the planners and the architects of post-war Britain that hooked me. The simple and fundamental idea that people need to be housed, and housed in decent, affordable, well designed and often beautiful homes.

When faced with the desire of living somewhere bigger a couple of years ago, I only ever contemplated living in a modernist home. With the reality of a modest budget, for London, it was obvious that it would most likely be ex-council, and so began a journey of discovering more and more fascinating estates in my city. Searching online for modernist properties on the market became a daily ritual. I can't remember how the idea came about, but I decided to compile my research on to a blog, including archive material, films, books, literally everything I was finding, mainly as a reference for my own purpose. It was soon apparent I wasn't alone in finding this architecture inspiring. In the first month alone I received 4,000 visitors. This later led me to begin a series of interviews with residents living on estates, asking questions and taking photographs to gain an insight into who these people were, and to get an insider's view of what their estate was like to live in. Again, this seemed popular, and my inbox began to fill up with either fan mail or proud estate residents wanting their home to be featured.

Having gone through decades where post-war, especially concrete, architecture has been vilified, I hope this is a sign of a new generation of appreciation for Britain's best housing of the twentieth century.

'Living in a high-rise block does not force all its inhabitants to become criminals, but by creating anonymity, lack of surveillance and escape routes, it puts temptation in their way and makes it probable that some of the weaker brethren will succumb.'

Introduction

So wrote Alice Coleman, geographer at King's College London, in her infamous 1985 work *Utopia on Trial*. This book marked the nadir of the reputation of the UK's stock of modern houses, built sporadically between the world wars and in massive numbers in the thirty years after. Coleman and her team, under the influence of Jane Jacobs' odes to the 'ballet of the sidewalk' and Oscar Newman's theories of 'defensible space', ran round London housing estates counting instances of graffiti, litter and pissy lifts, and decided that modern housing was all wrong, urban planning was impossible, and that the 'natural selection' of the free market meant little homes with little gardens were a way of living that was impossible (maybe even immoral) to improve upon.

Thirty years on, and Coleman's tirade against communal housing is clearly and obviously risible, and there were plenty of people who said so at the time. But *Utopia on Trial* perfectly ventriloquised the attitude to housing of that era's establishment, and it remains a testament to just how far common sense opinion had changed from the heady optimism of the 1960s. From a source of welfarist pride, hand in hand with the National Health Service, by the 1980s modernist and in particular council housing had been stigmatised so thoroughly that it was possible for Thatcher's government to practically end its construction altogether. As far as housing was concerned, architects were aloof, engineers were incompetent, planners were completely misguided, contractors were spivs, councillors were on the take, the whole thing was a god-awful mess, and only the steady miracle of 'what people really want' – meaning suburban cul-de-sacs built by developers – could rescue the industry.

But beyond all this, one startling thing remains true: the post-war period in housing was one of the very few times in history that Britain has been at the cutting edge of architecture. UK architects may not have been the initial innovators of new forms of housing, and they may not have been the most prolific, but they led the world in a number of ways. In the years after the war, a great many architecture students undertook pilgrimages to the European mainland, and especially the south of France, where they went to see Le Corbusier's Unité d'Habitation, one of the first major European post-war buildings, and the primary source for much of the world's high-rise housing of that era. Upon graduation, the best jobs were frequently to be had in local government, and inspired young men and women joined organisations like the London County Council, where new thinking was very much the order of the day, and estates like Alton West experimented with various European ideas – slab blocks, point towers – for the new era of housing.

As time went on, a new generation upped the level of experimentation further. Under the influence of the iconoclastic Alison and Peter Smithson, who had only recently been their tutors at the Architectural Association, Jack Lynn and Ivor Smith designed Park Hill. Supervised by Lewis Womersley at Sheffield City Council, this sprawling complex of more than a thousand flats challenged the Corbusian orthodoxy and endeavoured to recreate the positive spatial character of traditional working class housing, while simultaneously eliminating the horrible aspects of slum-living. Spiralling down from a position overlooking the centre of Sheffield, this complex famously incorporated 'deck access'. Better known as 'streets in the sky', this was an approach whereby flats were entered from communal platforms running through the estate, an attempt to mimic the social spaces that existed in front of slum flats, and was judged to be an improvement on the dark central corridors of the Corbusian model.

Architects, planners and politicians from all over the world came to study Park Hill, and its organisational innovations would be recreated again and again, not only in the gargantuan Hyde Park flats which rose yet higher on the hill behind, but all across the UK over the following twenty years, if rarely with the same aplomb as that which had been first achieved in the 'Socialist Republic of North Yorkshire'.

Another import from abroad, and perhaps the one which genuinely contributed most to the bad reputation of modern housing, was the introduction of system building techniques into British housing. In the years following the Second World War the housing situation remained critical, with bomb damage scarring the cities and millions of people still living in appalling conditions. The major political parties offered ever increasing targets for the amount of homes they would build a year, with the Macmillan government even offering increasing financial incentives the higher a tower block was built. At the same time, new developments in pre-fabrication originating from Denmark and France offered a way to drastically accelerate the production of homes. By building self-supporting concrete panels under controlled conditions in a factory, the labour involved in construction could be reduced, as all that was needed on site was to fix the panels together. All through the sixties, large areas of the UK were remodelled with towers, slabs and ziggurats, linked together by elevated walkways which separated pedestrians from the vehicle traffic below.

For a while at least, due to the three-dimensional urbanism being pioneered along with new towns such as Cumbernauld and their town centre megastructures, British architecture was at the cutting edge of housing design, more innovative than other, both more capitalist and socialist, countries. But typically, this just meant that there was further to fall. The Ronan Point disaster of 1968, where a gas explosion caused the progressive collapse of a panel-built tower, and its aftermath, when it was found that contractors had been fudging their work in ludicrously dangerous ways, marked the beginning of the end for advanced British housing. Over the next twenty years the system-building boom unravelled, as estate after estate was found to have been seriously bodged. Rain ran down the inside of walls, vermin infested entire blocks, black mould appeared everywhere, concrete fell off the walkways – a litany of ineptitude meant that, in some cases, estates had to be demolished after less than twenty-five years.

Furthermore, the sudden rise in the crime rate that occurred from the end of the 1950s onwards set people on a search for causes, and one potential culprit was the new housing environment that had been created up and down the country. By 1972, when the Smithsons were finally given their chance to build an example of their housing theories, at Robin Hood Gardens in Poplar, they were filmed by B.S. Johnson lamenting the vandalism that would be likely to affect their new housing when it was finally built. Throughout the economic crises of the 1970s, newly built estates with few facilities and uniformly disadvantaged residents risked becoming desperate zones of no escape, and the number of housing estates that gained a nickname such as 'Alcatraz' is testament to that. The police often identified the raised decks as a particular threat to safety, considering the way in which they provided multiple pathways throughout an estate, a perfect means for criminals to escape. The death of PC Keith Blakelock during the 1985

Broadwater Farm riots, caught by attackers utilising the raised decks for an ambush, helped fix this view of the three-dimensional city as a threat.

Wolmesley's successor to Park Hill, the system-built Hulme Crescents in Manchester, were effectively abandoned by the council before being demolished in the early 1990s, while large system-built estates like the Ferrier in south-east London, or the Heygate in Elephant and Castle, have now also been swept away. Those that remain, stigmatised still, are frequently earmarked for demolition, such as Robin Hood Gardens, or the vast Aylesbury Estate in South London, once the largest estate in Europe, whose council tenants are knotty inconveniences to be removed for the benefit of property investors.

With all this in mind, why is it that a book like this can exist at all? One partial explanation is that throughout all of these trials, there were still estates which shone through. Although there are indeed those who find Chamberlin, Powell and Bon's Barbican inhumane, its rugged hammered concrete has stood the test of time brilliantly, and now stands as a remarkably concise statement of the overall vision for modern housing – well built houses with expert design making the most out of the limited space of high-density living, leisure and cultural facilities as integral parts of the overall vision, and the romantic scene of greenery growing all over the rocky outcrops of the buildings, 'towers in the park' as a synthesis between nature and the man-made.

Of course the Barbican is an outlier, whose central location and hefty service charge, not to mention the ridiculous London property values, mean that it may well be a model, but is by no means typical. But literally across the road, the earlier Golden Lane Estate by the same architects remains more than 50 per cent inhabited by council tenants, suggesting that it isn't the wealthier residents that make the difference. Indeed, where they haven't been falling over themselves to sell off homes to developers, some council estates are where the ideal of mixed communities finds its most clearly positive examples, with vulnerable tenants, working families and the more affluent design-hungry residents all living side by side.

The architectural works which most clearly demonstrate the power and quality of the British contribution to housing were built in North London by the Camden Council Architects' Department. Under Sydney Cook, from the mid-1960s they created some of the most sophisticated and accomplished housing estates in the world, under very challenging conditions. Again, the models came from abroad, but what these young designers created using them is astounding. From the late 1950s, a new stop on the architectural tour of Europe was a small settlement outside of Bern, Switzerland, called Halen. Developed and built by the Swiss practice Atelier 5, this housing estate turned many Corbusian ideas on their head, while retaining a total commitment to modernity. Halen is an experiment in high-density housing that remains resolutely low-rise, with densely packed family houses arranged around communal facilities. What British architects realised was that these ideas could allow for a synthesis to occur between the ideas and aims of modern housing, and the traditional urban patterns whose intrinsic worth was becoming more and more cherished.

What Cook and Camden, and architects such as Neave Brown, Gordon Benson and Alan Forsyth, or Peter Tábori achieved, were new estates which fitted closely into the existing urban fabric, while also increasing the amount of green space and number of trees on the site. They managed to recreate established street relationships, with every house having a front door, while simultaneously separating pedestrians from the cars underneath. The flats themselves use space ingeniously, with large balconies, sliding internal partitions, full height windows and other intelligent planning strategies, while in daily life, neighbours greet each other on the walkways, and the children play outside unsupervised.

This sounds idyllic, but in many cases it was hard fought over. Most of the Camden estates were on site right at the point of the 1973 oil crisis, and the stories of their construction are more often than not fraught. Contractors went bust, poor workmanship had to be destroyed and rebuilt, costs ballooned far above the stringent benchmarks set by the governments. But in many ways this was thought a price worth paying.

One of the most emblematic of the Camden estates, Branch Hill, by Benson & Forsyth, is known as the 'most expensive council housing in the world'. It was in a number of ways a pure provocation – in 1964 the left-wing council acquired a large house and its land, right in the middle of affluent and leafy Hampstead. Turning the house into a care home, they intended to build council housing on the gardens, but were restricted by a covenant explaining that any construction had to be semi-detached, and no more than two storeys. Instead of suburbia, however, the Branch Hill Estate is a series of split level modernist houses on a grid of pathways, which ingeniously provide a large open garden on the roof of the neighbouring houses as they step down the hill, a defiantly communal gesture.

When Branch Hill was finally finished and tenanted in the late 1970s, the Architect's Journal noted that in such a transformed social environment the estate marked the tensions between 'Brave New World in contrast to Loss of Nerve'. By that point, there was no political will in the UK to create any more modern housing, and it wasn't until the late 1990s that high-density urban housing returned, in a vastly different form. Branch Hill, like the other Camden estates, Alexandra Road and Fleet Road, has now been listed, the establishment belatedly recognising its historic significance, but no housing of this quality, designed for ordinary people, has been built since.

But what is it, precisely, about these homes that appeals? Of course, ultimately, there is much that boils down to an element of taste. There are those who have the money to make the choice, for whom yet another Victorian terrace is of no real interest, and the flowing spaces, expansive glazing and modernist planning of high quality post-war housing fits perfectly with an interest in modular furniture, Swiss graphic design, perhaps a bit of atonal music and abstract art as well. This may well account for much of the attraction for many of the people featured in this book (this author included), but underneath this stylistic question there are deeper cultural issues, about who builds housing and for what purpose, about the role of technology in the fabric of daily life, and about how humanity should address the future. Modernist housing is the result of an era in architecture of soberly optimistic considerations of what humans were capable of, and how they might live together, and the dreams of the period can still be sensed in the concrete of its houses.

Douglas Murphy

Isokon

Belsize Park
London

Architect
Wells Coates

In the early twentieth century, in the wake of the aftermath of the Industrial Revolution, housing in Britain's towns and cities was often poor and overcrowded. In the 1930s, architects escaping the Nazi regime in Germany joined forces with British architects and began to re-imagine housing for a new and clean modern age. With a shortage of homes, the building of flats was being encouraged by local authorities and this resulted in a few Bauhaus-influenced experimental buildings popping up across London. The Isokon in Belsize Park was the first block of flats in Britain to be built in the International Modern style.

With its sculptural access balconies the Isokon looks like a stranded concrete ocean liner. It stands on land bought by Molly and Jack Pritchard. They commissioned the flamboyant architect Wells Coates (1895–1958) to design a new type of accommodation for communal living aimed at young professionals who had little time for housekeeping, or as described by F. R. S. Yorke in *The Modern Flat* (1935), 'One room and two room flats for bachelors'. Services such as shoe and window cleaning, bedmaking and dusting as well as furniture designed specifically for the flats were all included in the annual rent of £96.

The Isokon contained a total of thirty-one flats plus quarters for the staff, kitchens and a garage for ten cars. It was constructed in reinforced concrete with steel windows and doorframes, plywood dadoes and linoleum flooring. Heating and hot water was supplied to each flat from a central plant in the basement. In 1936, two years after the initial opening, the communal kitchen was replaced by the Isobar restaurant, designed by the Bauhaus architect Marcel Breuer, where avant-garde intellectuals and artists would meet. This would all have been incredibly modern and progressive, but perhaps it was ahead of its time as this type of communal living never really took off and the post-war period witnessed the building's steady decline. The Pritchards became unable to carry out the expensive and comprehensive maintenance it needed and in 1973 it was eventually taken over by Camden Council. The English Heritage listing granted in 1974 meant that the council also struggled to properly maintain the building, and it fell further into disrepair.

Luckily in 1999 the Isokon's fate changed when Camden Council announced a competition for the restoration of the building. The winning team was made up of the Notting Hill Home Ownership, Avanti Architects, with Alan Conisbee Associates as the structural engineers, and the Isokon Trust who began to meticulously restore it in 2003. Additional flats were incorporated where the staff quarters had been – sympathetically in keeping with the original design of the interiors. By 2004 most of the restored flats were sold to key workers on a shared ownership basis, and in order to cross-finance the works the bigger flats – including the glamorous penthouse which had been the Pritchards' flat – were sold on the open market.

Opposite
The Isokon flats, photographed from the entrance on Lawn Road in 1934

Sharon Keane

London-born Sharon is a digital project manager with an obsession for analogue cameras and photography. She lives in a one-bedroom apartment on the ground floor of the Isokon that she bought just over a year ago.

Tell us a bit about your home
The building is dazzling in the sun and glows in the dusk. Most people think it's white but it's actually painted in a subtle shade of rose pink. Being minimal the flats are rather cosy, but cleverly designed to make the most of the available space. So many buildings are built with no thought for the person that has to live in them. The Isokon is the opposite – it was created for living. It's such an inspirational place to come home to, I still pinch myself to check that I really live here.

What's the area like?
Hampstead Heath is a five-minute walk and Primrose Hill is not much further, which is such a pleasure. I love running so having two of the best parks in London on my doorstep is an incredible luxury. The area is full of independent butchers, bakers and (probably) candlestick makers. But everything shuts by 5pm on a Sunday, which takes some getting used to. I used to live in Bethnal Green, so Hampstead can feel a bit too civilised sometimes. The Isokon itself is surprisingly quiet – I can sit in the garden, surrounded by trees and squirrels and feel a million miles away from the double decker buses and grey suits of the city.

Since its refurbishment, has the building been well maintained?
Of course there are grumbles about things not being done, but generally the Isokon is a wonderful place to live. The gardens are kept trim, with almost military precision – I've lost a few herbs to over-zealous strimming. The building is surrounded by trees, there's a nature reserve behind it, so there's a daily battle with leaves and twigs falling, but that's part of the charm. When she lived here, Agatha Christie wrote about watching the big, white, cherry tree on the bank from her window every morning – it's one of the many that still surround the Isokon. The Grade I listing also means you

can't knock down walls but in a one bedroom flat you'd struggle to find a wall worth removing anyway. You're also not allowed to remove any of the original D-handles from the doors, which means all the flats still look pretty much as Wells Coates specified in his original plans.

What are the neighbours like?
Those I've spoken to are really friendly. We have a residents' association so I've met a few people through that. Most people living here own the flats so it feels quite settled and everyone looks after the place, which is great. There's a distinct lack of families and children because of the size of the flats, which I'm quite happy about. And there's not been a communal bar or restaurant since the 1930s so there are no wild parties!

Best things about living here?
Clearly I love the modernist design of the building, especially the enormous windows, which make my lounge feel a bit like a viewing platform in a rainforest. There are hidden cupboards and shelves everywhere. One of my favourite things is a built-in bookcase which covers an entire wall in the hallway. Another is the fact that my bedroom used to be the laundry room. I recently discovered that the laundry was once responsible for losing Agatha Christie's knickers. It was quite a scandal. She wrote to complain and her letter was kept as part of the building's archives.

Worst thing about living here?
It's really cold in the winter. I moved in during possibly one of the coldest weeks I've ever experienced and the heating broke on the second day. It's an old, concrete building with big windows, so it's never going to be energy efficient.

Finally, if money were no object, where would you live?
Right now I wouldn't swap my flat for anything. But, if my book collection continues to grow at its current pace, and I can persuade my girlfriend to move in with me, then a bit more space might be nice. In which case, I could be tempted by one of those Highpoint penthouses in Highgate by Berthold Lubetkin.

Above
The restored original facade colour (a very pale pink)

Above
The kitchen was sympathetically
built to match the original design

Above
The hallway with built-in floor-to-ceiling bookshelf

Above left
The bedroom

Above right
The bathroom

Pullman Court

Streatham
London

Architect
Sir Frederick
Gibberd

One of the most significant housing schemes of the 1930s to fully embrace modernist principals is Pullman Court in Streatham, South London – an area that was already home to good quality accommodation for young professionals. The scheme was built on three acres of land which had previously been used as a tram depot. It was acquired by the developer William Bernstein who commissioned the young architect Frederick Gibberd (1908–1984) who was a mere twenty-three at the time. It was Gibberd's first major work. He later went on to specialise in the design of flats and was subsequently the master planner of Harlow New Town.

The initial designs for Pullman Court met with considerable opposition, not only because of its unusual modern appearance, but also because of the concerns that housing for single people, which would be primarily men, would encourage prostitution. As a result larger units for families were incorporated into the development consisting of 218 flats varying in size from one to three-rooms. The flats were aimed towards the middle classes and despite a great deal of them being on the small side, they were marketed as a combination of luxury, labour-saving and stylish living. Services offered included a restaurant, a social club, a swimming pool and lock-up garages. Rents ranged from between £68 to £130 a year.

The layout of the scheme was mainly determined by the long narrow site and by the desire to minimise the impact of the adjacent main road. There was also the requirement to retain as many of the existing trees as possible. Pullman Court comprises five three-storey direct access blocks fronting Streatham Hill, two five-storey gallery access blocks along the central driveway and two seven-storey cruciform blocks at the rear of the site overlooking the covered reservoir of the Lambeth waterworks, all arranged around a landscaped setting. The buildings were constructed with a reinforced concrete frame, panel walls and flat roofs. Internally there was an exceptional level of detailing and refinement – the modern streamlined kitchens came with built-in refrigerators, there was ample built-in storage, a wireless loudspeaker cabinet, and an electric fire as a focal point in the living rooms all designed by Gibberd himself.

Today the buildings are painted a crisp modernist white, however the original colour scheme was surprisingly bold with a range of warm browns and beiges on the road front, to cool white and blues to the rear, and there are long term plans to restore the exterior to its original colours. Pullman Court was listed Grade II in 1981 and later raised to Grade II*.

Opposite
Pullman Court, photographed
from Streatham Hill in 1938

Eva Tyler

Eva has been living in her two-bedroom near-original apartment in Pullman Court for more than twenty-eight years. She is currently studying for a master's degree.

Did you know much about Pullman Court before you moved here?
I didn't know anything. When I first walked up the driveway between the blocks I got the vibe. It was a wreck then but still a very satisfying space.

What attracted you to living here?
The flat seemed to be all windows with built-in storage in every room, and it felt very large – the double-width hallways and all those windows make it feel bigger than it actually is.

Are the buildings well maintained?
Beautifully. When I moved in, the block was on the buildings at risk register. A lot of hard work and a lot of investment has brought it back to life and there's no going back. We have a team of caretakers and a managing agent who are rigorous about keeping the site in good condition and work with the residents on improvements. Each year we pay into a reserve fund and save up, so the major works we've needed to do haven't been a shock.

Is there a good community here?
It's an interesting, mixed crowd. Some people have been living here longer than I have and there are plenty of younger folk who have moved in for the architecture. We participate in Open House each year, and I open my flat mainly because I seem to have the most original features. Gibberd designed all the fittings and what I didn't find when I moved in I've cannibalised from what other people have thrown away when they've refurbished their flats. So I've got all the original door handles – chrome Ds and mushroom knobs – some lighting, radiators, electric fire and so on. The knocker on the front door is a small delight. The block is often used as a film location and for photo shoots, it's got that modernist photogenic quality, good gardens and views from the roof.

What are the best things about living here?
My flat works for me and is always a pleasure – today the sun is pouring into my living room. Plus, I'm in the back block, so it's quiet, but good transport links are just at the end of the drive.

Worst thing about living here?
The flats can get damp if you don't ventilate well. The old airbricks got blocked up years ago and the flats weren't designed for modern heating systems.

Finally, if money were no object, where would you live?
Nearer to Vitra and Ronchamp.

Above
The hallway with the living room ahead, kitchen
and bathroom to the left, and bedrooms to the right

Above
The main living room with the original linoleum flooring

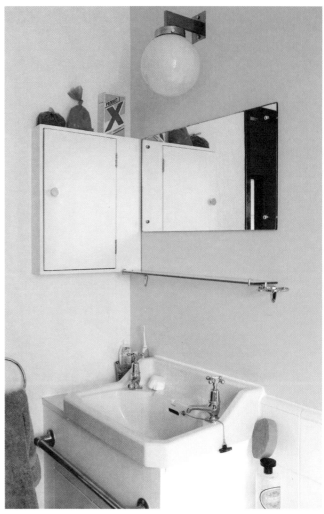

Above left
The near-original kitchen

Above right
The bathroom with the original light fitting designed
by Gibberd and produced by Best & Lloyd Limited

Opposite
The master bedroom

CUTHBERT HARROWING HOUSE

Golden Lane Estate

City of London

Architects Chamberlin, Powell and Bon

The interwar years saw very little housing being built in Britain, and by the time the Second World War ended in 1945 it had left huge scars across the country. The bombing had either destroyed or made uninhabitable one million homes, and, coupled with the number of Victorian slums, there was a major housing shortage. All the political parties agreed that an ambitious reconstruction programme was needed and optimism to build a better Britain was in the air. Aneurin Bevan at the Ministry of Health and Housing wanted to provide council homes for a cross section of society. In urban areas high-density solutions were seen as necessary but the standard for public housing was initially very high, despite the shortages of materials and rising inflation.

In the middle of the nineteenth century over 130,000 people lived in the City of London, but by 1952 that number dropped to just 5,000. A series of architectural competitions for housing schemes gave great opportunities to Britain's best young architects and were a good advertisement for ambitious local authorities seeking to construct high-density, low-cost modern housing.

The City announced the competition to design an estate at Golden Lane in 1951 on two hectares of a heavily bombed site on the southern border of Finsbury. The competition attracted 178 entries, including 'streets in the sky' solutions by Alison and Peter Smithson who later went on to design Robin Hood Gardens in Poplar. The winning entry by Geoffry Powell (1920–1999) – who had previously worked for Frederick Gibberd – was a much more humane design with three- and six-storey blocks around a central courtyard and a high-rise tower as a centrepiece. Powell joined forces with his colleagues Peter Chamberlin (1919–1978) and Christof Bon (1921–1999) and together commenced on their first housing project.

Like many of their contemporaries, Chamberlin, Powell and Bon were heavily influenced by Le Corbusier and in particular his Unité d'Habitation in Marseille which was completed in 1952. There are many 'Corb touches' in Golden Lane Estate, not least the 'cowboy hat' concrete canopy on the roof of the tower, Great Arthur House (pictured), with its pergola and water garden for the residents and spectacular views across the city (unfortunately this was closed in 1981 following a suicide).

The architects embraced an innovative approach to design, rejecting the traditional urban forms such as streets lined with houses. The scheme comprises a total of nine blocks and is a true urban environment – incorporating shops, a pub, a community centre, a swimming pool, a children's playground, bowling green (now tennis courts), courtyards, a fish pond and underground car parking. The first phase of the estate was officially opened in 1957 with the last phase completed in 1962. The estate was popular from the beginning and the first residents to move in included an architect, policemen, nurses and teachers.

Internally the flats are modest in proportion but the spaces are cleverly designed with the use of sliding partitions, cantilevered stairs and double height glazing to maximise space and light. The estate was given Grade II listed building status in 1997 with the exception of Crescent House which is Grade II*. Many flats are dual aspect with windows looking at the deck access balconies or the courtyards, making the estate a very open and social place with a strong sense of community.

Opposite
The fifteen-storey tower and maisonette blocks of Golden Lane Estate, photographed from Fann Street shortly after completion in 1957

Matthew Carter

Actor Matthew has been a Golden Lane Estate tenant since 2001. Renting from the City of London, he lives in a one-bedroom flat in Grade II* listed Crescent House.

Did you know much about the estate before you moved here?
I knew it was designed by the same architects as the Barbican, and the Barbican had always been one of the places I'd aspired to live in.

How did you manage to get a flat in sought after Golden Lane Estate?
I was renting privately in the City in 1995 and the council (the Corporation of London) sent me a letter telling me that as a resident in the City I was eligible to rent one of their council properties – I just had to fill in a form and return it to them if I was interested. So I did, and a year or so later I heard back saying I'd been offered a flat in Bermondsey, in their Avondale Square Estate. I immediately took it. I then found out I could go on a transfer list if I wanted to move to another City of London estate. So I applied to be transferred to Golden Lane Estate. I was warned I would be waiting some time as no one leaves Golden Lane Estate unless they die, but eighteen months later they offered me this flat.

Describe your flat
Originally it would have been a studio flat with a separate sleeping area, but the person who was here before me put a wall up and turned it into one bedroom, which actually works better for me. The bathroom is original, but the kitchen was also redone at some point and the original listed partition dividing the kitchen and living room was taken away, which I'm thinking of reinstating.

What's it like having the council as a landlord?
That's a hard question. I feel very lucky to live here but in some ways they are a little short sighted. For example, the government's recent Decent Homes Standard policy meant that all the flats (aside from those belonging to leaseholders) had their kitchens and bathrooms updated. Even though this place is listed they just ripped everything out and rather than being sympathetic to the original designs, replaced them with kitchens and bathrooms that looked like they had been in a time capsule since 1985. Which makes them sound nice but they weren't.

What about the communal areas, are they well maintained?
I would say they are pretty well maintained. It's kept clean, but 'just' clean. A lot of the flats are sublet through private landlords and it feels that some of the people who live here don't know or care about the importance and history of the building.

What are the neighbours like?
The neighbours are nice. It's very much a mix of people with about 50 per cent leaseholders and 50 per cent tenants, and on the whole everyone is very friendly. It's quite a strong community and we hold regular events like summer fetes and Christmas markets. There are a few people who have been here since the estate was built.

What are the best things about living here?
Obviously the architecture, and the facilities on the estate are excellent, we've got a swimming pool here, a gym and tennis courts. And the location is fantastic – the Barbican Centre is on our doorstep, and I can walk in to town in twenty minutes.

What are the worst things?
The short sightedness of the landlord, although they are trying to change. We have regular residents' meetings, it's a slow progress but they are starting to take into account residents' feelings.

If money were no object, where would you live?
That is really tough – there are so many places I would like to live. But perhaps in Connecticut, where there are tons of modernist houses, or an Eichler house in California.

Above left
The dining area with original parquet flooring

Above right
The main living space looking toward the front door

Opposite
View of part of the living space

Opposite
The bedroom with view of the tower,
Great Arthur House, from the window

Above left
The kitchen

Above right
Exterior view of Grade II* listed Crescent House

Keeling House

Bethnal Green London

Architect Sir Denys Lasdun

The East End of London suffered particularly badly from both bomb damage and Victorian slums. It had been an area with strong ties and values but these were beginning to disappear as communities were being broken up. In an attempt to retain these ties architect Sir Denys Lasdun (1914–2001) wanted to design something different to the typical slab blocks with single storey flats that were being built by local authorities in the 1950s. He stood the traditional Victorian Street on its head by placing maisonettes on top of each other to create a 'cluster block'.

Lasdun studied at the Architecture Association and later worked with Wells Coates before joining Berthold Lubetkin and Tecton. The influence of Coates and the Modern Movement is clearly evident in his work. After serving as a Major in the Royal Engineers building airfields for Allied fighter squadrons during the Second World War, he set his attention to rebuilding Britain. Lasdun wanted to give the people in Bethnal Green light, spacious homes with privacy and a balcony – yet retain a sense of the neighbourliness and community they were used to in their old homes. In a cluster block all the noisy services such as the lifts, rubbish chutes, stairs and drying platforms are placed in a central core, which has maisonette units grouped in four pairs around it. Having a small footprint, Keeling House required the demolishing of only six houses therefore avoiding disruption to the existing street pattern or character. Completed in 1959 the building stands at sixteen storeys high, all the flats are maisonettes except on the fifth floor (the maximum height of a fireman's ladder) where there are studio flats. Each maisonette had a spacious lounge, kitchen, pram store, two double bedrooms and a bathroom upstairs. For the residents who had come from slum housing with only outside toilets this must have felt like complete luxury. The building is made of reinforced concrete with precast cladding of Portland stone finish. Lasdun was heavily influenced by 1930s modernism and Keeling House's proportions are more elegant than the majority of blocks built at that time. He designed a similar, smaller, block a few years earlier at Usk Street, also in Bethnal Green, and both buildings proved popular with the residents.

By the 1980s, however, structural problems began to surface and the precast cladding began to fall apart. Despite the council, Tower Hamlets, spending £1.2 million repairing it, by 1984 the problem was getting worse. Cracks began to appear in stairs and in 1991 a Dangerous Structure Notice was served on the building and the residents were forced to move out. Tower Hamlets could ill afford the £4 million estimated cost to repair Keeling House and earmarked it for demolition. However, defenders of the building fought to save it and in 1993 it was Grade II* listed – the first tower block to be given such status. Tower Hamlets had no choice but to sell it on the open market. It was bought in 1999 by private developer Lincoln Holdings, for £1.3 million, who commissioned Munkenbeck and Marshall, with the approval of Lasdun, to refurbish it. The flats were modernised, a lobby and concierge added and the structural problems fixed at a cost of £4 million. They were then all sold to the private sector marketed towards young professionals.

Opposite
Keeling House, photographed
shortly after its completion in 1959

Paul Harfleet

Paul Harfleet is an artist and is best known for his work on 'The Pansy Project', a campaign to plant a single pansy at the site of homophobic abuse around the world. He is currently working on an illustrated children's book. He has been living in a two-bedroom flat in Keeling House for six months.

Did you know much about the building before you moved here?

When I used to live in Bow I would walk past Keeling House on my way to Columbia Road Flower Market and covet the building. After Bow I moved to West London for a while, but I wanted to move back to the East. It is completely fortuitous that I'm living here now. My current flatmate was in New York last year and was looking for somewhere to move to in London. She saw this flat advertised online and told me about it, and I was like 'I love that building!', so I came to view it. The landlord was great and I loved it immediately, so she trusted me to take it without her even seeing it.

Is the building well maintained?

Yes, what really makes a difference is that there is a concierge here during the week, from 9am to 5pm. He keeps track of everything. The lift is mopped every morning, the communal spaces are all kept clean. It's not high-end glamour – but it's very efficient and clean and tidy.

What are the neighbours like?

I lived in a council tower block in Manchester for eleven years, which I loved and I ran an artist's led space from there, but it did have slightly less salubrious residents. There would be crack addicts and prostitutes in the lifts frequently. This place is very different. You can tell that everybody that lives here is very proud of the building.

What's the best thing about living here?

When I'm in my room, watching a programme or whatever and I glance out of the corner of my eye and see the skyline, you see the buildings, and the weather coming towards you – it's amazing. I love my walk to work and I love coming home. It's that feeling of 'I can't believe I live here'.

What are the worst things about living here?

The rooms are perhaps slightly on the small side, although absolutely adequate for two people, but (and this would be terribly ostentatious) I would love to live here on my own! If I were to be really picky, although it really doesn't bother me, because the building is Grade II* listed, the windows are single glazed so it can get a little chilly in the night. It hasn't felt unpleasant though, and when the sun shines it floods into the rooms and heats the flat up and is bright all day.

Finally, if money were no object, where would you live?

Here! I'd love to be able to buy here, but I don't think I will ever be in a position to do so, it's just one of those things – but I'm just about able to afford to rent here. I've got the work/life balance just right so I feel incredibly lucky.

Opposite
Open plan kitchen and living space

Above
Living space with glazed door to the balcony

Above left
Looking into the kitchen from the hallway

Above right
The landing

Above left
One of the two bedrooms

Above right
The bathroom

The Hall
Blackheath
London

Architect
Eric Lyons

Private housing after the Second World War had mainly followed layouts and designs of what had gone before with traditional, conservative and unimaginative designs that did not reflect the mood of the post-war Britons who hankered after a new and better way of living. Modern architecture was reserved for either council estates or for the wealthy who were able to afford one-off houses.

Architects Eric Lyons (1912–1980) and Geoffrey Townsend (1911–2002), who met during the 1930s while studying at the Regent Street Polytechnic in London, had a keen interest in modern architecture, Lyons having previously worked for Walter Gropius and Maxwell Fry. The duo saw a market for well designed, affordable, modern family houses built on a larger scale and together they formed an architecture practice before the war. However, their vision to build a new kind of housing was met with reservations by developers who were afraid of trying anything new. In a bold move, in 1953, the duo decided to set up their own company, Span Developments, to design, build and sell the houses themselves. Townsend had to resign from the RIBA as at that time they did not allow members to act both as architect and developer. He would act as developer and Lyons as Span's architect.

They went on to build some 2,100 homes in seventy-three developments between the 1950s and 60s in the South of England, a vast majority of them in Blackheath, where Span acquired a number of small sites on the Cator Estate. The unmistakable Span design with its monopitched or flat roofs and high standard of detailing such as tile hanging and weather boarding, although distinctly modern at the time was also very humane. Internally the houses felt open and light with large glazing in the living rooms.

Landscaping was a key element to Span estates. They rejected the more standard pattern of estate layout and its relationship to roads. On the majority of Span estates the roads are private, which allowed them to control the materials for the paving, which softened and unified the overall schemes. Pedestrians were given priority. Instead of parking being directly outside each house, Span produced separate car parks and 'car squares' that were screened by planting. The layouts of the houses and flats were carefully designed around lawns and courtyards. The residents were encouraged to take an active role in the running of their estate, each being managed by a Residents' Committee.

Span Developments proved a popular experiment in modern living, but their most ambitious and controversial development, New Ash Green in Kent, would eventually see the company's financial collapse. The scheme was meant to be a mix of private and socially rented homes built by the Greater London Council, but in 1969 the GLC pulled out. Nevertheless, Span did succeed in launching a modern way of living for the twentieth century and similar housing was replicated (mostly with less success) across the country. The estates have stood the test of time, today Span homes are highly desirable with a number of the developments Grade II listed.

Opposite
T2 Span houses at the Hall,
Blackheath, photographed
shortly after completion in 1960

The Wells

Liz and husband Mason live in an immaculately refurbished T2 Span house on the Cator Estate in Blackheath with their two daughters Meg and Daisy. Liz runs a small paper goods company, Dicky Bird, and Mason is a partner at graphic design studio Bibliotheque.

Describe your home
[Liz] The house itself is small and open plan with large windows. It was in a bit of a state when we moved in; most of the original fixtures had gone and there was an extension with no foundations. Mason worked with the architects of our previous apartment, KMK Architects, who helped us with a simple scheme, using basic materials that complemented the Span feel.

How long have you lived here?
We moved here in 2003, when Meg was two. Previously we lived just off Old Street, and although we loved city living, things like trees and grass were hard to come by. Lugging a pram up four flights of stairs was no fun either.

Did you know much about Span before you moved here?
We knew a bit, but the RIBA's Span exhibition in 2006, and the accompanying book gave us a lot more information. We were attracted by the classic Span elements – the big open spaces and well thought-out landscaping and found that you could get a lot more for your money by buying a mid-century house compared to the more 'desirable' Victorian or Georgian stock.

What's the area like?
It's a really interesting area. There are so many different types of architecture going on, you often see groups of architecture students wandering around. On the Cator Estate alone there are Georgian terraces, Regency villas, a council estate, a variety of Span estates, pre- and post-war houses – as well as some really interesting individual buildings like 10 Blackheath Park designed by Patrick Gwynne, and number 20, designed and owned by Peter Moro until he died in 1999. Blackheath Village is a good mix too, sitting between urban Lewisham and Royal Greenwich.

What about the communal areas, are they well maintained?
We are lucky to have a big grassy area, called the Green, where most of the kids on the street hang out and play. There's a great swing hanging from a huge cedar tree in the centre and a small play area. We pay an annual fee towards the upkeep of things like roads and pavements and the maintenance of the gardens.

What are the neighbours like?
All sorts, although you do tend to get a lot of designers and architects. When we first moved here, there were still a few people left who had lived here since 1958, but most of them are now no longer with us. Lots of people say that these houses are too small, but plenty of people have raised whole families here.

What are the best things about living here?
The space. Meeting other like-minded people. You really do get to know everyone on your street. It's very peaceful. When we first moved here, I remember sitting on the end of the bed and listening – and I could hear absolutely nothing! After Old Street with its 24/7 traffic and sirens, I was amazed.

What are the worst things about living here?
The aluminium roof blowing off our house right before Christmas last year and us ending up living at the Premier Inn for a month (and then two more in a rented flat in Deptford). But now we have a beautiful new roof and it should be good for another fifty-six years!

Finally, if money were no object, where would you live?
We often talk about moving back into the city when the girls have left us. A massive modernist apartment in Marylebone could be nice!

Above
View of the main living space from the kitchen

Above
View of the porch and stairs

Above left
Exterior of the back of the house

Above right
The kitchen

Above left
The original wall that separated the stairs
and the living room has been knocked through
to create a more open space

Above right
The bathroom

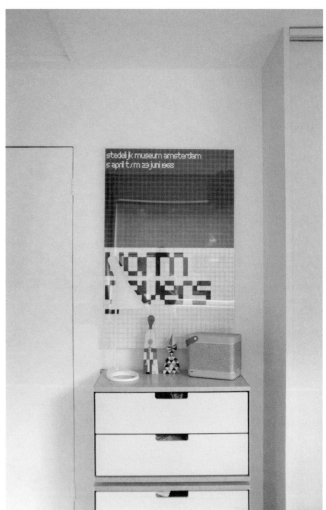

Above left
Meg's bedroom

Above right and opposite
The master bedroom

Dulwich Wood Park Estate

Crystal Palace London

Architects Austin Vernon and Partners

The Dulwich Wood Park Estate is a mixed development of terraced houses and high-rise flats, nestled in a peaceful woodland hillside setting in Sydenham Rise. The land had previously been home to large houses which were in poor condition. After the war the land owners, the Dulwich Estate, were under increasing pressure from the government to use the land for council housing in order to help with the shortage of homes and increase the population of the area. The Dulwich Estate resisted and proposed that they would redevelop the land themselves.

Austin Vernon and Partners were appointed architects for the estate and after several revised plans a mixed scheme with a density of fifty persons per acre was finally approved in 1957. Wates construction company, who had recently completed a project in the area, were appointed to build the development within three years. The scheme was highly innovative for this time, following Corbusian principles of clean, healthy housing in a green parkland, but visually it was altogether much softer – drawing upon Scandinavian designs rather than Le Corbusier's Unité d'habitation. The architects maximised the open space and preserved the existing trees to maintain the ground in park-like condition. The landscaping was of extremely good quality, designed by the highly regarded landscape architect Derek Lovejoy.

The first phase of the project consisted of terraced housing and three blocks of eight-storey flats. The second phase was a mix of 120 terraced houses and six nine-storey blocks of flats. The houses were modern with open plan rooms and split levels between the dining and living room. Externally they looked very different to traditional terraced housing, with decorative tile hanging and timber boarding not dissimilar to Span's designs.

The flats were marketed to the professional classes, the sales brochure boasted of well-equipped kitchens with power points, refrigerators, scarlet Formica worktops, elegant bathrooms, built-in furniture and tropical hardwood floors. One of the best features were the full-width windows in the living room with magnificent views of the city. The expensive fittings were not restricted solely to the flat interiors; lobbies were fitted with Terrazzo flooring and glazed wall tiles, and lifts clad in patterned Formica. It was the height of luxury and modernity. They proved extremely popular, with reports of prospective buyers camping outside the showroom flat on the day they were released for sale. The estate received a Civic Trust award in 1964 and was widely praised in the architectural press.

Today the estate remains very well looked after. Its green setting and relatively affordable prices (compared to central London) are attracting a new breed of residents, young families with an appreciation of its design, which will hopefully ensure its future preservation.

Opposite
The original pergola entrance to Knoll Court, the first block to be completed on the Dulwich Wood Park Estate, 1960

Jim Green

Jim is a senior children's book designer. He lives in a two-bedroom flat on the second floor of Marlow Court, one of the high-rise blocks, which he bought four years ago.

Did you know much about the Dulwich Wood Park Estate before you moved here?
I didn't know anything about the estate until I started looking in the area. I had a tip off from the chap who cuts my hair that Crystal Palace and its environs had some hidden gems.

What attracted you to living here?
I have always liked modernist style housing. As a kid I had friends that lived in Harlow New Town in these amazing Span influenced houses and I guess it stuck in my subconscious growing up. Being a child of the seventies that general vibe pervaded lots of the world around me. I think a main turning point for me as an adult was going to the Robin and Lucienne Day retrospective at the Barbican about thirteen years ago. From that point on I knew exactly the sort of aesthetic that excited me, and how I would like my house to look. A few years later I was fortunate enough to buy and live in a 1960s house in Kew and the interest went on from there. After briefly renting in the Barbican three years ago I moved to south-east London and the search started from then to where I am now. The continuous deep window in the living room, with its original metal frame, was for me the main attraction of the flat.

What's the area like?
My flat is surrounded by large trees and is very peaceful. There's communal ground all around the estate and families sit out there in the summertime and have barbecues and picnics. I am right next door to Crystal Palace which is a really friendly and diverse neighbourhood, lots of good eateries and pubs and also some very well priced antique dealers. As a keen runner I am also surrounded by some superb parks. Crystal Palace Park has some amazing views southwards and of course the dinosaurs! A short jog downhill and I am in Dulwich Park, and Herne Hill and Brixton are just a short bus ride away.

Is the estate well maintained?
The grounds are kept immaculate and the communal halls and stairs are cleaned every morning. There's a strong emphasis with residents on keeping the blocks in their original condition which in general seems to be happening.

What are the neighbours like?
Really lovely, my next door neighbour is a retired teacher and is often inviting me round for gin and tonics and a chat. There's a nice mix of ages here including young families. Everyone I have spoken to loves living here and many have been here for ten years or more.

What are the best things about living here?
The giant window and the views of the trees outside. I have a resident woodpecker that seems to like the oak tree outside my bedroom and I even have a tawny owl hooting sometimes. Connections are excellent – I can get into central London quite easily, plus, with the overground line at Crystal Palace, I can get to Shoreditch High Street in about twenty-five minutes.

What are the worst things about living here?
The wooden floors are quite creaky and I can hear my neighbour upstairs walking about quite loudly. I guess they hear the same from me below. Television noise travels through the floors a lot.

If money were no object, what would be your dream home?
Tricky one as I keep discovering new modernist delights in this city. I have no intention of moving out of London so maybe the most obvious and extravagant choice would be a flat in one of the Barbican towers. However, being a practical person, one place that caught my eye recently is nearby in Sydenham, quite a modest residence in Peckerman's Wood by the same architects that designed my flats.

Above
The living space with full-width windows

Above
The dining space

Above left
The kitchen with the original sliding door

Above right
The hallway with the bedroom ahead
and the kitchen to the right

Above left
One of the two bedrooms

Above right
Communal corridor

Manygate Lane

Shepperton Middlesex

Architect Edward Schoolheifer

The houses at Manygate Lane are somewhat of an anomaly and feel out of place in the quiet village of Shepperton in Middlesex. Few developers aside from Span managed to successfully deliver modern housing for the private sector, but Manygate Lane is a fine example of experimental British housing. The developer behind the scheme was the flamboyant Ronnie Lyon. Son of a builder he started his career by making and selling garden sheds. By the 1950s he had developed simple, steel-framed industrial buildings and made his first million by the time he was thirty. He began to expand his business into other areas including the subsidiary company Lyon Estates in the early 1960s.

Their first housing development was the Wheatlands Estate in Heston, Middlesex completed in 1963. It comprises 195 dwellings ranging from town houses to flats in an eleven-storey tower arranged around landscaped lawns and communal gardens, designed by Swiss architect Edward Schoolheifer. Shortly after Wheatlands, Schoolheifer was commissioned, again by Lyon, to design housing for middle to high income families at Shepperton on land bought by the Lyon Group in 1962, which had previously been home to nineteenth-century villas. The estate was built in three phases and includes 80 terraced houses, completed in 1965. Their designs were more radical and modern than the previous Wheatlands Estate, with huge floor-to-ceiling glazing, open plan living, flat roofs and integrated car ports arranged neatly around two landscaped courtyards. The houses sold for a premium of £7,695 each at a time when the average London home was £3,500. With its close proximity to Shepperton Studios a host of celebrities opted to live there, including Marlon Brando, Rod Steiger, Julie Christie and Tom Jones (there are some fantastic press photographs of him lounging around his pine clad living room).

After their sixties' heyday the houses began to look a little tired, with residents making a number of unsympathetic changes. Following a residents' campaign to preserve the original features of the estate, Manygate Lane was designated a Conservation Area in 2002. Today it is home to a mixed community, including those looking for interesting family homes within travelling distance to London without the price tag Span estates demand.

Opposite
The two-storey houses which wrap around the landscaped courts, photographed in the 1960s

Tim Bubb

Tim, a dealer specialising in mid-century Scandinavian furniture and part-time horticulturist, lives in a two-bedroom, two-storey townhouse with his wife Akiko and three-year-old son Alex.

Describe your home
The house faces south with pretty much the whole front elevation glazed. There are some lovely features such as spiral staircases and a good size balcony straight off the lounge. I suspect this is one of the most original houses left on the estate. We still have the original aluminium windows at the front and nearly all the fixtures inside. I spent a lot of time stripping white gloss from all the internal wooden features when we first moved in.

What attracted you to living here?
I must have stumbled upon some images of the estate online as I had been here several years before we moved in to have a wander around and take some pictures of the architecture. One of the residents noticed me taking an interest and invited me in for a look round. I bookmarked the place in my brain as I was very impressed with the boldness and quality of the architecture. Good quality mid-twentieth-century modernist housing estates like this are few and far between in the UK.

Are the communal areas well maintained?
Yes, very much so. The gardens are impeccably kept and really create a sense of calm, with the larger houses arranged around two rectangular lawns and gardens. There are lovely walkways through the estate which are gently lit at night. There is a very healthy proportion of green space allotted and it is one of the key ingredients which make it a success in my eyes. We lived on a Span estate prior to moving here which had a very similar relationship between the landscape and the buildings.

What are the neighbours like?
There's a mixed bag of age groups. I have noticed that the most recent arrivals to the estate have a keen interest in design and have set about restoring their houses sympathetically and true to the original design, which is really encouraging.

What are the best things about living here?
The light – even on a dull winter's day the house is bright and airy. Summer evenings when you can roll back the lounge door and sit with a glass of wine watching the parakeets (yes, parakeets) in the branches of the trees opposite. I also enjoy the house at night, the light bleeds from one level to another creating a calm and mellow effect. The design of the houses are very different from most people's preconceptions of what a house should look like. I remember not long after we moved in, a couple walked past outside and I overhead one of them say, 'Oh, what horrible houses.' This made me smile.

What are the worst things about living here?
We have the original aluminium single glazed windows on the front which I would never consider even for one second changing as they are so beautiful. However, they do let the outside noise in. Luckily it is a very quiet area but occasionally you will experience some noise, especially in the summer when the windows are open. Also, the design of the house is not ideal for small children. We have had to be very creative with baby gates to make the place safe.

If money were no object, where would you live?
I don't know. It would probably have a mono-pitch copper roof, there would be shuttered concrete exposed in places and an internal courtyard.

Opposite
Exterior view of the three-storey
terraced houses

Above
The living area and balcony

Opposite and above left
The bedroom

Above right
View from the living space of the spiral staircase
leading down to the hallway, and open stairs leading
up to the bedroom

Opposite
The living space with original parquet flooring

Above left
1970s bathroom

Above right
The ground-floor kitchen

Park Hill
Sheffield
Architects Jack Lynn and Ivor Smith

Known locally as 'Little Chicago' the pre-war Park Hill area of Sheffield had a notorious reputation for its high levels of crime. Slum clearance began in the 1930s with a pause during the war and became one of the biggest and most ambitious inner city redevelopments of its time. It was chosen for its close proximity to Sheffield's City Centre and its sloping hillside location. Sheffield's city architect Lewis Wormersley commissioned Jack Lynn (1926–2013) and Ivor Smith to design a scheme which would retain existing communities and rehouse entire streets.

Inspired by Le Corbusier's Cité Radieuse in Marseilles, Lynn and Smith introduced the 'streets in the sky' to Britain – snake-like interconnected Brutalist buildings ranging from four-storeys to thirteen-storeys with a continuous roofline. It contained some 994 flats for 3,000 people with three-metre wide open deck access big enough for milk floats or for children to play – encouraging neighbours to interact with one another as they might on a regular street. Because of the sloping site each deck had access to the street at some point. The blocks were constructed using concrete frames infilled with brick in a progression of warm colours.

Shops, pubs, a school, children's play areas and seating were all integrated into the scheme. It was important to ensure the least possible disruption to the community, so old neighbours were housed next to each other and the familiar original street names used. Community development officers helped residents settle in and the project was given extra government funding which meant standards were higher than in other schemes by local authorities. The flats were light and generous in proportion, each with its own balcony and fantastic views over the city. Twelve caretakers lived on-site and were on 24-hour call. It was officially opened in 1961 and was extremely successful becoming a showpiece of social housing.

By the 1980s the local steel industry in Sheffield collapsed and caused mass unemployment. This saw Park Hill descend into dilapidation and soon become a no-go area overrun with crime. The pubs were boarded up, cars burnt, walls graffitied, drugs rife and the secluded walkways became a target area for muggings. The concrete fared less well in the colder, wetter climate of Yorkshire than in Marseille and began to spall. People complained of noise and poor insulation, of lifts breaking down and the Garchey refuse disposal which was prone to getting blocked. It became the embodiment of the 'sink estate' and rather than presenting an idealistic view of the future, it came to represent all that was wrong in post-war concrete architecture and social housing.

Park Hill divides opinions – loved by some and hated by others, with great controversy it was listed Grade II* in 1998 (the biggest estate in Europe to be listed) and its fortunes began to change. Fashionable property developer Urban Splash took over the building and commissioned architects Hawkins\Brown and urban designers Studio Egret West to renovate it. Everything except the concrete frame of the old building was removed. The coloured brick infills were replaced with a new facade of aluminium panels in red, orange and yellow. The flats were made bigger, with a metre taken away from the width of the deck access, and windows looking over the 'streets in the sky' were added to make them more sociable spaces.

The redevelopment has brought new life to Park Hill but the majority of the original council flats are now in private hands. The council has stipulated that one third of the 900 new flats will be 'affordable' but with a mere 200 available for social rent. The first phase has now been completed and received a Stirling Prize nomination in 2013.

Opposite
A typical bridge connection between blocks at Park Hill, photographed shortly after completion in 1961

Katy Caroll

Katy and her husband bought their flat on the recently refurbished Park Hill nearly two years ago. Both lecturers at Sheffield Hallam University they divide their time between here and their second home in Stockport, Manchester.

What did you know about Park Hill before you bought here?
I studied Art and Design History (specialising in graphic design and architecture) and was introduced to the flats by Hilary Grainger, who was one of the architectural specialists on the course. I've been lecturing in Art and Design History since graduating and have often included Park Hill in my lectures – it's almost become compulsory since I've been working at Sheffield Hallam!

What made you decide to move here?
After deciding to stop commuting and to live in Sheffield during the week, the opportunity to live here was one we were quick to take. We are both big fans of modernist architecture, it is incredibly convenient for work, and it gives us an opportunity to live in a different way – our other home is a 1903 terrace house.

Are the renovated buildings being well maintained?
Maintenance is currently limited due to the development project still being in the early stages, but the communal areas we have access to are very well maintained, and always clean. Part of our service charge contributes to a sinking fund (for any future structural work, including the roof) – we saw this as a positive feature, as it hopefully means we won't have any future problems with the building or selling our flat on.

What are the neighbours like?
Great, there's a real mix of people, and this was one of the things we considered beyond our love of modernist architecture when we bought the flat – some of the neighbours have been living on Park Hill since its earliest days.

What are the best things about living here?
Concrete! The interior/exterior space, the views afforded by the wall of floor-to-ceiling windows (at both the front and back of the flat) and the light they bring right into our living space. At the front we overlook a roundabout used by trams, cars, bicycles and pedestrians. It has trees and greenery in the centre, a swimming pool on clear view through the glass roof, and trains running alongside into the station; it's constantly moving. At the back we see the original Park Hill flats, in all their glory, juxtaposed against some of those that have been 'urban splashed'.

What are the worst things about living here?
Beyond its close association with work, how often the windows get cleaned. We have an amazing view, it would be good to see it all year round. It can be noisy – we had to get used to the traffic at the front – but I'd miss all that action if it weren't there.

Finally, with money no object, where would you live?
Marcel Duchamp's old home, Lincoln Arcade Building, near Central Park in New York.

Above left
View into the dining area from the bedroom

Above right
View into the bedroom from the dining area

Above
Part of the living room

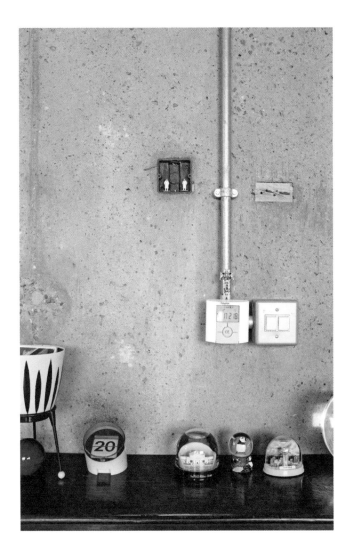

Above left
Some of the original light patresses have
been retained and left on show

Above right
View of the stairs from the hallway

Above left
The landing with exposed concrete walls

Above right
The bedroom

Above left
The kitchen

Above right
View of the old Park Hill buildings
yet to be refurbished

Opposite
The 'streets in the sky'

Sivill House
Bethnal Green London

Architects Skinner, Bailey and Lubetkin

The pioneering architect Berthold Lubetkin (1901–1990), a Russian émigré, believed 'nothing is too good for ordinary people'. He moved to Britain in 1931 after a decade travelling Europe and studying in Paris. He brought with him optimism for a better future as well as a new type of architecture. Shortly after his arrival in London he set up the Tecton Group with six graduates from the Architecture Association, including Denys Lasdun. There were very few buildings in the International Style in Britain at this time and one of Lubetkin's first commissions (as part of the Tecton Group) was for luxury housing in Highgate – Highpoint I and II (completed in 1935 and 1938), which were highly praised and now widely regarded as the finest examples of modernist architecture in the country.

In 1935 Tecton were commissioned by Finsbury Borough Council to design a health centre. The building was created with the intention of improving public health. There was no National Health Service at this time so the concept of such a building was very progressive. For Lubetkin, who believed his work, art and architecture as a whole should help shape and reflect social change, the Finsbury Health Centre was an ideal commission.

Tecton's relationship with Finsbury continued and in 1943 they were appointed to devise an urban plan for the reconstruction of the borough and went on to design three housing schemes: Spa Green (1943–1950, Grade II* listed), Priory Green (1943–1957) and Bevin Court (1946–1954, Grade II listed). Many of their ideas, developed for the luxurious Highpoint apartments, were applied to inexpensive council housing.

Disillusioned by the conservative level of post-war commissioning, the Tecton Group dissolved in 1948, but Lubetkin continued to work on housing projects including Sivill House in Bethnal Green, with two other Tecton members, Francis Skinner (1908–1998) and Douglas Bailey (1915–1977). The fifty-nine-metre, twenty-storey building stands proudly on Columbia Road in East London and was the last phase of the ambitious but less successful Dorset Estate. Built between 1951–1957 the design of the initial phase of the estate had to be revised from its original proposal of three modest and openly spaced blocks to two larger eleven-storey Y-blocks. The second phase saw the inclusion of maisonette blocks and finally, in 1964, Sivill House.

Built on a cleared site of the old Columbia Square model dwellings of Baroness Burdett-Coutts, the building feels both visually and physically detached from the rest of the estate. According to Skinner it was included at the insistence of the London County Council Housing Department. The striking facade is typically decorative akin to Lubetkin's other work, with concrete C panels inspired by Caucasian dragon carpet design to enliven what would otherwise be a monotonous front. The building is actually made up of two blocks with angled plans and roof grids linked by a circular tower housing a dramatic spiral staircase – a Lubetkin speciality. He believed that the communal areas should have a level of grandeur and more social importance – this also resulted in better lighting and greater privacy for the flats.

Opposite
Exterior of Sivill House, viewed from Columbia Road

Andrea Kettler

Born in Austria and raised in Ireland, Andrea (pictured with partner Sam Jacob) has been living in London for the past fifteen years. She studied astronomy, went on to become a journalist and now works for a Shoreditch-based PR company. She lives in a one-bedroom flat on the fifteenth floor of Sivill House that she bought nearly four years ago.

Did you know much about Sivill House before you moved here?
I run a blog about council housing in London and Sivill House is actually the first building I ever wrote about, back in August 2009 when I was living in Bethnal Green. As a result I knew a little bit about its history.

What attracted you to living here?
The main thing was the affordable price of the flat for the area and the fact that it was in a friendly, well designed block.

Are the communal areas well maintained?
Yes, they are. Although I would say this is down to the hard work of the residents, rather than the management organisation. In particular we have one amazing tenant, Spencer, who does more for Sivill House than the rest of us could ever thank him for. He's a superstar!

What are the neighbours like?
I have found everyone to be really friendly. On my floor there are two families with young children, and a man lives in the flat next to mine. He had an awesome party on the opening night of the 2012 Olympics, complete with views of the whole park and the fireworks!

What's the area like?
It couldn't be a lovelier. It's on Columbia Road where the street comes to life every Sunday with a buzzing flower market. There are also two ace pubs, the Royal Oak and the Birdcage, which hosts infamous Friday night karaoke.

What are the best things about living here?
The block has a beautiful concrete-panelled facade. At its heart is a spiral staircase and each floor has four flats, all of which are triple aspect and with a balcony.

Mine is on one of the higher floors and faces west, so my view looks out over London as far as Battersea Power Station, Wembley Stadium, Alexandra Palace and the Crystal Palace television antenna. It's generally quiet and feels like a little oasis in the middle of London. You really can't beat the location.

Worst thing about living here?
When both of the lifts break down it's a long way up the stairs. Luckily, that's only happened once since I've been here.

Finally, if money were no object, where would you live?
In London, it would be Ernö Goldfinger's house at 2 Willow Road in Hampstead.

Above
The living space

Above
The dining area with the balcony beyond

Above left
The kitchen

Above right
The bathroom with mosaic tiles which
mimic the facade of Sivill House (not original)

Above left
The communal spiral staircase

Above right
View of the Dorset Estate, from the balcony

Balfron Tower
Brownfield Estate

Poplar
London

Architect
Ernö Goldfinger

The Balfron Tower in Poplar, East London, forms a striking and forceful silhouette on the London skyline. The twenty-seven storey Brutalist tower block was designed by architect Ernö Goldfinger (1902–1987), a Hungarian émigré with a reputation for being strong willed. After studying in Paris at the École nationale supérieure des Beaux-Arts in the 1920s, Goldfinger moved to London, and to a flat in Berthold Lubetkin's Highpoint in Highgate with his wife, an artist, Ursula Blackwell. In 1937, using Ursula's trustfund, Goldfinger designed a group of three houses in Hampstead, the middle and largest of them for his own occupation. The flat-roofed concrete-framed houses were met with substantial local opposition. Despite seeming very modern at the time, they were actually fairly restrained and sympathetic to their surroundings, with graceful Georgian proportions, and are now much admired.

Goldfinger's approach was new, experimental and bold. By the early sixties he was at the height of his career having completed a number of projects including private housing, schools and Alexander Fleming House in Elephant and Castle. It wasn't until 1963 that he was finally asked to design his first large-scale public housing for the GLC. The Balfron Tower forms part of the Brownfield Estate built in an area of London where the houses had either been devastated by the Second World War or were so run down that they were uninhabitable. Standing at 276 feet, its height was seen as a positive by Goldfinger – building high would create more open space on the ground and give the residents fantastic views from their homes over the city. Noisy services were separated away from the flats by way of a separate lift tower, joined to the main residential block with bridge-like walkways constructed of reinforced concrete. The flats themselves were spacious and light-filled with quality fittings, and designed with great attention to detail.

Shortly after the Balfron was opened, Goldfinger and his wife moved into one of the flats at the top of the tower for two months to gain first-hand experience of living in the building. They opened their home to the other residents, hosted drinks parties and quizzed them about what they thought of the building. Ursula kept thorough journals throughout this time and noted that after meeting the tenants they 'all said the flats were lovely'. Based on his stay at the Balfron, Goldfinger went on to make improvements to the design, such as including an additional lift, in his later Trellick Tower in West London.

Catastrophically, in 1968, three months before the Balfron was officially completed, came the Ronan Point disaster. A gas explosion on the eighteenth floor of a system built tower block made the whole side of it collapse. Four people were killed and seventeen injured. This disaster, alongside growing social problems blamed on high-rise buildings, such as isolation and rising crime, would see architects like Goldfinger and tower blocks in general vilified.

A lack of proper maintenance over the years took its toll on the building, and when it was Grade II listed in 1996 Tower Hamlets found it increasingly difficult to look after. Ownership was transferred to the housing association Poplar HARCA and residents were promised a number of improvements. It was soon apparent, however, that the refurbishment needed would require all the tenants to move out and the initial option for them to be able to return to their homes was removed. Instead, the renovated flats would be sold off privately. Some have supported the decision, making the point that the money made from sales will be reinvested into social housing, but others are see it as gentrification and social cleansing. The flats are currently being let on a short term basis to artists and property guardians who provide the building with some security.

Opposite
The Balfron Tower, photographed in 1965, shortly after its completion

Maria Lisogorskaya

Maria is co-founder of Assemble, a collaborative practice of artists, designers and architects. She has been living on the twenty-fourth floor of the Balfron Tower for the past two years.

Describe your home
I live in a one-bedroom, single-storey flat. The living room is generous, as is the balcony, which is accessible from my bedroom as well as the living room. The flat is west facing and the balcony's built-in planter box is much better than those ugly slick glass balustrades.

How did you come to live here?
The opportunity came about because of the planned development of this previously social accommodation into private apartments. Poplar HARCA, the housing association who own the building, have been decanting the building for the past few years. I'm renting the flat on a short term basis through Bow Arts – one of the organisations which provides low cost live/work spaces.

Did you know much about the building before you moved in?
I knew about Goldfinger and the Balfron and Trellick duo. I've always wanted to live high up, and I am a fan of Brutalism and the generosity and intelligence of residential layouts designed at the time. When referring to social housing in London, the high-rise has often been demonised; meanwhile thousands of new luxury residential towers seduce the councils and are marketed privately.

Who else lives in the building?
Bow Arts tenants like myself, other short term tenant organisations such as Dot Dot Dot, and some remaining Poplar HARCA residents, though most of them have been decanted by now.

What are the communal areas like?
The community cabin downstairs is great, they run dance classes, community gardening, and there's a 'pub' upstairs. The huge lifts are also good places to bump into people, the journey is just long enough to have a quick conversation.

What's the area like?
The Brownfield Estate which Balfron is part of, is in a residential area between the towering Canary Wharf, industrial low rise of the Lea Valley and the Blackwall tunnel. Chrisp Street market is nearby and great for vegetables. There was a lovely flower shop which used to have a parrot greeting you, but it recently closed due to the council's changing of rent conditions. You can't get a flat white here (yet).

What are the best things about living here?
The layout, the view and my neighbours. Plus it's affordable, although not for much longer!

What are the worst thing about living here?
Having to leave, and all the people who have had to leave due to the 'glamorisation' of Brutalism. The poor level of housing provision in this area and the exclusive developments that have little architectural merit make for an unbalanced regeneration. Also, being perceived as 'a tool of gentrification' in this regeneration process, when in reality there are few housing opportunities I can afford. Affordable homes, in the real sense of the term, don't seem to exist in gentrified areas.

If money were no object, where would you live?
I would build an interpretation of a Case Study House on top of a skyscraper overlooking the Thames. Or on top of the Shard.

Above
The main living/dining space

Above
View of the door to the balcony from the living space

Above left and right
The bedroom

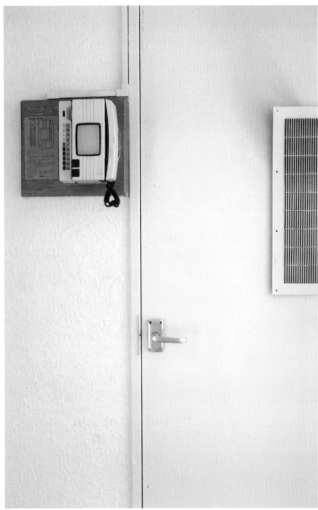

Above left
View of the hallway as you enter the flat

Above right
Door entry phones were installed in the 1980s
and featured a CRT monitor

Perronet House

Elephant and Castle London

Architect Sir Roger Walters

Over a third of the buildings in Elephant and Castle – a neighbourhood that was already deprived and suffering from bad infrastructure – were damaged during the Second Word War. The London County Council reconstruction programme saw this as an opportunity to plan a comprehensive regeneration of the area. In the 1950s, after several revisions, an ambitious masterplan was finalised that would include housing, offices, a shopping centre, a printing college, and an improved road network with two new roundabouts.

The first phase saw the completion of the new road layout. In an era when the car was king, pedestrians would now navigate the roundabout by a network of subways. One of the first buildings to be erected was the Michael Faraday Memorial on the north roundabout – an electricity substation clad in shiny aluminium panels. The largest self-contained arcaded shopping centre in Europe, designed by architects Boissevain and Osmond, was completed in 1965. Ernö Goldfinger's Alexander Fleming House, a government office building (now luxury flats) and a cinema (now demolished) were completed in 1967 and set the precedent for the Brutalist aesthetic in Elephant and Castle. It was soon apparent however that the segregation of cars and pedestrians was not ideal. The subways were unwelcoming and confusing, access to the shopping centre was difficult and by 1966 only half of the shops were occupied.

The next three decades would see the unpopularity of the Elephant and Castle grow, in particular with the press. The shopping centre went through a couple of reinventions, and although popular with local residents and businesses it failed to become the 'Piccadilly of the South' it was intended to be. In the year 2000 a major new redevelopment of the area was proposed, which would see the majority of the 1960s buildings, including the Heygate Estate which was home to 3,000 people, swept away and the land sold off to developers for luxury glass towers aimed at foreign investors. As part of a £1.5 billion scheme, the shopping centre will also be demolished and replaced with a pedestrianised market square and green open spaces. It is all too easy today to criticise the architecture of post-war Elephant and Castle, its buildings are often slated as concrete monstrosities, but the planners' ambitions cannot be so readily dismissed. The area had to be radically rebuilt and reinvented and they did so with optimism for a positive and better future and (unlike today's property developers) did so for ordinary local people.

One notable building to have survived the developers' bulldozer is Perronet House. It was built by the LCC in the late sixties and designed by Sir Roger Walters (1917–2010), who had studied at the Architecture Association in the 1930s. He pioneered the now routine practice of 'public consultation', encouraging colleagues to explore what he described as 'a mutual understanding between architects and those for whom they build'. The block contains seventy-two flats at a density of 170 persons to the acre. In May 1970 the first residents moved into the building and the following year it was commended in the government's national Good Housing Awards for its 'boldness and conviction'.

Opposite
Elephant and Castle, looking west, from the shopping centre to Saint George's Road and Perronet House, 1970

Ben Mason and Emma Allen

Ben and Emma live in Perronet House on the north-west of Elephant and Castle roundabout. Ben bought the flat in 2007, and Emma joined him a couple of years later. Emma is an artist whose work ranges from body painting, animation and sewing to making some of the wall pieces and furniture you can see around the flat while Ben has recently started his own food business and has launched a range of 'proper baked beans'.

Tell us a little bit about your flat

[Ben] Perronet House's most distinctive feature is only apparent once inside one of the original flats. All are split over five levels with rooms split over three. The maisonettes interlock in manner known as 'the scissor section'. This design minimises communal space and maximises living space. Some flats go up from their entrance, some flats go down. All have their living room and kitchen at the front for morning sunshine and the bedrooms to the rear, away from the noise of the roundabout, whilst the bathrooms and communal corridors are tucked away in the centre of the block. Ours is a one-bedroom flat which we did some fairly substantial work to in 2010. We removed three internal walls and a false ceiling to increase the sense of space in the living area and bathroom. The flats here are really light and spacious.

Did you know much about Perronet House before you moved here?

A friend of mine and now tenth-floor neighbour, Richard Reynolds, was renting a sixth-floor flat when I was looking to buy a flat. He was my introduction to the block and a huge help in taking the leap into tower block living. I was totally sold on the flat from the minute I walked in. It was twice the size of anything else I'd looked at and the walls of windows hooked me in immediately. I was looking in the Elephant and Castle area because I wanted to buy somewhere central but on a tight budget.

Are the communal areas well maintained?
They're not bad for a large block in such a busy location. Southwark Council, our landlords, are not that good at maintaining the block – but the tenants' and residents' association has become quite adept at keeping tabs on them.

What are the neighbours like?
Lovely! We're very close to some of our neighbours and on first name terms with all of them on our floor and many other residents. Friends of ours call it 'the commune' because there's so much interaction between neighbours.

Best things about living here?
Space, light and friends for neighbours. And being in the Elephant, of course – zone one's dirty little secret.

Worst thing about living here?
Southwark Council

Finally, what's your dream home?
It's hard to see us leaving Perronet House. But we have a dream of building a beach house in Sri Lanka. There's some incredible modernist architecture there, much of it by Geoffrey Bawa. And the climate allows houses where inside and outside blend into one. It's not uncommon to have a hole in the ceiling so the rain can pour in through the middle of a living room.

Above
The dining area, looking out on to
Ernö Goldfinger's Metro Central Heights
(originally Alexander Fleming House)

Above
The living space

Opposite
The dining area with full-width windows

Above left
View of the living room as you enter the flat

Above right
View of the stairs

Above
The kitchen with original serving hatch

Above
The bedroom

Above left
The hallway with built-in storage

Above right
The bathroom

Barbican Estate

City of London

Architects Chamberlin, Powell and Bon

The City of London boasts one of the most radical post-war mixed schemes ever to be built. Standing on a site which had been devastated in the Blitz, the 'Barbican area reconstruction plan' was conceived in 1947 by architects and planners Charles Holden and William Holford. Their vision for rebuilding the City was very different to how it was finally realised – they planned for a predominantly commercial district with new roads, office areas, pedestrian walkways but very little housing. By 1952, however, the City's population had plummeted, and concerned that without an electorate there would be no local autonomy, the City of London Corporation set about revising their plans to incorporate residential buildings.

Chamberlin, Powell and Bon, who were already working on the neighbouring Golden Lane Estate, were selected to work on the masterplan for the Barbican area. The brief was to build a mixed scheme with housing for 330 people per acre. By 1959 the final plan, which incorporated schools, leisure and cultural facilities, shops and a mix of low-rise residential blocks and towers was approved, but it wasn't until a year later that Chamberlin, Powell and Bon were appointed to design the buildings themselves – and even that was on the proviso that the Corporation could bring in other architects if they deemed their designs unsuitable.

The three striking triangular tower blocks stood thirty-floors in the original plans, but were increased by fourteen floors in the final design, allowing for more open spaces between the buildings, making them the tallest residential buildings in Europe at that time. Pedestrian walkways, formal residents' gardens reminiscent of Georgian squares, a picturesque lake complete with a waterfall and fountains, all at varying levels, created order without monotony. Pedestrians were elevated onto highwalks, separating them from the dangers and noise of the traffic below (an idea which was originally planned to be built across London but never fully realised). The architects initially planned to clad the buildings with marble (imagine!) but was later rejected in favour of pick hammered raw concrete – giving the buildings a solid and unified look, visually similar to the later blocks of the Golden Lane Estate. Semi-engineered brick was also used below the podium level to echo the materials of the buildings that had previously stood there.

A total of 2,113 flats and housing for 6,500 people was built, aimed at middle to high-income residents, based on the fact that the units needed to attract rents high enough to cover the commercial value of the sites. The majority of the housing was either one or two bedroom for what the architects described as 'young professionals, likely to have a taste for Mediterranean holidays, French food and Scandinavian design'. To attract these potential wealthy residents, car parking for 2,500 cars, district heating, Garchey refuse disposal systems and a theatre were all incorporated into the design. Internally the spaces were luxurious, well built with quality fixtures, lots of light and space, often utilising double height ceilings and full height picture windows leading out to terraces or balconies.

In 1964 the City decided a larger theatre and concert hall would be more financially viable than they had originally planned. This became the Barbican Centre, one of Europe's biggest art centres, and was officially opened by the Queen in 1982.

The first residents moved into the Barbican in 1969, but by the 1980s Brutalist architecture had become synonymous with social housing and it fell out of favour, drawing a host of critics declaring it Britain's ugliest building. Today the estate has had a huge resurgence. It was granted Grade II listing in 2001, and the properties are expensive and much sought after.

Opposite
Shakespeare Tower under construction, photographed in 1972

David McKendrick

David is the former Creative Director at *Esquire* magazine, and has recently launched his new design company B.A.M. He grew up in Clydebank in Scotland and has been living in London for fifteen years. He bought his studio flat in one of the low-rise blocks in the Barbican three years ago.

Tell us a little bit about your flat

It's a large style studio – a type F1D to be precise. I've partitioned the living and sleeping areas with the Vitsoe Shelving System which goes from floor to ceiling, and painted the concrete floor a nice industrial grey. The lease stipulates that floors are carpeted to prevent noise but as I live on the first floor with no one below me and I don't wear high heels, I think it's okay.

Did you know much about the estate before you moved in?

Yes, I used to live in neighbouring Golden Lane Estate about ten years ago, and I also rented a flat in the Barbican for a year. I tried living in Hackney for two years before I bought this flat but it just didn't compare. This area is just so unique and peaceful for London. The Barbican is in its own special little bubble.

Is the estate and your building well maintained?

It's always clean, tidy and very well kept. I pay quite a lot for service charges, which includes daily refuse collection – someone comes to remove my rubbish and recycling from a natty little two-way cupboard next to my front door every morning. Also the car park has twenty-four hour attendants that can hold or receive packages for you. The communal areas are great, especially the private gardens in the middle of the estate. It's like a secret garden. Only your flat key can gain you entrance and it's so peaceful and very well looked after – it's really good for people watching.

What are the neighbours like?

I don't see much of my neighbours, which I'm fine with. All the flats in my block are studios. I have a feeling they are owned by people who have a lot of cash and houses in the country and only use them weekdays. But the ones I have met are lovely, even if a wee bit nosey.

What are the best things about living here?

The location, peace and quiet, and the swimming pool a stone's throw away at Golden Lane Estate leisure centre – now that is London's best kept secret.

Worst things?

My flat overlooks Beech Gardens which has been a building site for the last year and we are looking at another two years of repairs before it's back to its lovely state. The City of London Corporation as landlords have been pretty slow at getting things done, I think there is a lot of red tape there and that cripples progress, as well as the fact that it is a listed building.

Finally, what's your dream home?

I feel like I already have my dream flat to be honest. It would be nice to have a separate bedroom but if I won the lottery I would definitely stay in the Barbican. I would like to stay here for the rest of my life and buy a penthouse in one of the towers – fingers crossed.

Above
The living space

Above
The dining area with sliding glazed door
leading to the balcony

Above left
The original Barbican kitchen designed
by yacht designers Brooke Marine

Above right
View into the bathroom

Brunswick
Bloomsbury
London

Architect
Patrick
Hodgkinson

It is difficult to imagine today that ten years ago the white futuristic ziggurat blocks of the Brunswick, in its upmarket location in Bloomsbury with its bustling shops and cafes, was a windswept area home to just a few down at heel shops. The building looked tired and the concrete was a drab grey and stained. Very few people would have chosen to live here. The way we find it today is much more in keeping with how the architect, Patrick Hodgkinson (b. 1930) initially envisioned it.

The scheme (then called the Foundling Estate) was conceived as a private development in 1958. Due to the shortage of housing, the government encouraged both local authorities and private developers to build more homes, and developers were given big subsidies to do so. On a site close to Russell Square, Georgian houses deemed unfit for living were cleared, and plans for redevelopment of the area which were to include housing, shops, entertainment and car parking for the upper end of the market were set in motion. After several rejected planning applications Leslie Martin, former Chief Architect of the LCC, was appointed, who in turn employed a young Patrick Hodgkinson as his assistant. By 1963 the design was approved and subsequently Hodgkinson was appointed as the main architect. The mixed scheme was unlike any other being built at the time. The trend for high-density housing was to build upwards, but Hodgkison's design was low-rise – two stepped blocks with a central piazza for the shops. His initial designs would have seen the buildings built from load-bearing brick, but this was later revised with the introduction of a concrete A frame carrying a tier of single aspect housing on each side. The flats were designed to be spacious and full of light with glazed balconies as winter gardens.

Just a year later, however, the future of the Brunwsick looked uncertain. The introduction of a new legislation by the Labour government in 1964 meant that the developer was now responsible for rehousing or paying huge compensation to the original tenants who had lived on the site. The developer, Alec Coleman, could ill afford to do this, so Hodgkinson suggested that he offered the housing elements of the scheme to the London Borough of Camden on a ninety-nine-year lease. In 1966 the deal was struck, but the high-end retailers such as Fortnum and Mason who had planned on taking the premises in the shopping centre, did not take well to the change of direction to council housing and most pulled out.

Budget cuts caused a number of revisions to be made. The flats themselves were made smaller in order to fit in more units, and with various other compromises to the quality Hodgkinson found it increasingly difficult to work on the project and finally resigned in 1970. Despite the final scheme being met with praise by both Camden Council and the architectural press, the estate fell into decline. Residents complained of severe maintenance issues and there were disagreements between the council and the freeholder about who was responsible. The future of the estate was again hanging in the balance. Several unsympathetic redevelopment plans were proposed during the 1970s and 80s, but in 1999 the fate of the Brunswick finally turned when it was bought by Allied London. They brought Hodgkinson back on board to upgrade the scheme with fresh landscaping and improvements to the retail units. The much needed painting of the blocks was finally completed in 2005. It was Grade II listed in 2000.

Opposite
View of the Brunswick from Marchmont Street, photographed in the 1970s

Vicky Richardson and Adrian Friend

Vicky works for the British Council in central London, where she runs the department for Architecture, Design and Fashion. She lives in a two-bedroom flat with husband Adrian Friend and their three daughters. Adrian is an architect and his practice has its studio in one of the units on the second floor of the Brunswick.

How long have you lived here?
[Vicky] We bought the flat back in November 2001. Our eldest daughter was one, and we had another on the way. The two youngest girls were actually born here in the flat.

Did you know much about the estate before you moved in?
I knew about it mainly because my dad was part of the design team – Patrick Hodgkinson had been his tutor at the AA. There was also David Levitt (who lives opposite us), David Bernstein and Peter Myers (who moved to Sydney to work on the Opera House). My dad was responsible for the cinema and the car park.

We'd always admired the building, and, on a practical level, buying a former council flat was also the only way we could afford to live in central London. It was very run down when we first moved in – the shopping precinct had a small supermarket, a charity shop, a couple of cafes, a second-hand bookshop and not much else. You'd often go to the rubbish chute and find a prostitute or addict in there. The external walls were a patchwork of different shades of paint, as many residents had painted away the exposed concrete.

Are the communal areas well maintained?
Yes, very well maintained. Our caretaker, Bah, lives upstairs and does a good job. There's a bit of an informal free-cycling system going on too – people leave unwanted things outside the lift and they soon get taken away.

What are the neighbours like?
Many of them are good friends now. About a third of the flats are privately owned, but the rest are council flats, some of them for sheltered tenants. Along from us are a couple in their nineties who moved here shortly after the building was completed. They speak vividly about how it felt like being in a posh hotel. There are quite a few architects here, inevitably, and more recently property developers, bankers and lawyers. Our girls like playing with friends down on the second floor podium, although there are a few elderly people who hate kids and like to shout at them.

Best things about living here?
I love the light and the feeling of connection to the sky. Internally the flats are very well planned. Most of all I love the building itself. I really do think it's one of the best and boldest pieces of architecture in the UK. The fact that several rows of Georgian houses were demolished to make way for the Brunswick, says a lot about the ambitions and optimism of the 1960s. I love the fact that it is a megastructure, and expresses the idea that all aspects of city life were provided for in one building, including housing, shops, doctor's surgery, workshops, cinema. I also enjoy the fact that the flats are almost identical, but the residents have adapted them and made each feel so different inside.

Worst thing about living here?
We keep being hit by massive service charges, and much of the work commissioned by the freeholder and the council has been shoddy – the contractor struggled with some historic flaws such as drainage pipes that are buried in the concrete. The renovation by Levitt Bernstein a few years ago has definitely revived the shopping precinct, and its great to see the place full of people, but the design of the new shops has the anonymous feel of an airport. All the glass and steel is not in the spirit of the original in my view. On a practical level, we need more space now the girls are getting bigger, and I'm yearning for a garden.

If money were no object, where would you live?
We'd like to buy the flat next door and knock through to make one huge flat, although that doesn't solve the problem of a garden!

Above left
The living room

Above right
The patio, originally conceived as a glazed winter garden

Above
The bedrooms

Opposite
The cathedral-like concrete A-framed structure

Byker

Newcastle-upon-Tyne

Architect Ralph Erskine

Byker is one of the most striking, as well as one of the last, large-scale social housing schemes to have been built in Britain. Barely one mile from central Newcastle it is a visual feast of colour and materials. With low-rise housing around courtyards, greenery and open space built on a hill site, it has a village-like feel. The estate is punctuated by the Byker Wall – a one-and-a-half mile-long block to the north of the estate that stands at twelve-storeys at its highest and three at its lowest, wrapping itself around the rest of the estate protecting it from the noise and pollution of the neighbouring main road.

By the 1960s old Byker had a population of 17,000 with streets of run down 'Tyneside flats'. A redevelopment plan was proposed and Swedish-based architect Ralph Erskine (1914–2005), having recently completed some private housing in Killingworth in Newcastle, was appointed. By 1968 Erskine's proposal for the redevelopment of the site was approved by the city council.

Keen to retain the strong family ties and sense of community, Erskine's scheme was unique and pioneering as it opened up a direct dialogue between the residents of Byker and the architects. He believed that architecture wasn't first and foremost involved in buildings, but in people, and out of their needs and desires, would come the architecture. Vernon Gracie, the resident architect, set up a site office in the old funeral parlour and maintained an open door policy where anyone could drop in to ask questions about the scheme or share any concerns they may have. Great efforts were made to involve the whole of the community with regular exhibitions, open meetings and clubs to create a fresh and inventive take on housing. Also unique was the retention of many of the existing buildings. Instead of insensitively flattening the twenty-acre site, buildings including the pubs, church and the swimming baths, as well as salvaged items such as railings and gates, were all designed into the scheme. There was a great sense of enthusiasm and innovation from both the architects and the community.

A pilot scheme of forty-six dwellings was completed in 1970 which provided the architects with feedback from the tenants. The Wall followed shortly after that, containing small units for childless residents and the elderly, and the first full phase of timber-framed houses began in 1972. The estate was officially opened by the Duke of Edinburgh in 1974 to rave reviews from the architectural press and indeed the residents. By 1980 however, delays in construction and a change in government caused the scheme, and Erskine, to fall out of favour with the local press and council, and the sites for the final phases were sold off to private developers.

As is so often the case, maintenance and bad management issues began to arise early on. The original community was changing and soon the traditional industries of the area, such as shipbuilding, were disappearing, seeing unemployment rise rapidly. The estate began to gain a bad reputation and became a very undesirable place to live. In 2000 an English Heritage listing application was rejected and there were drastic plans to demolish a number of the blocks. Things began to turn around for Byker however, with a conservation plan prepared by the North of England Civic Trust in 2002 and an estate wide three-year upgrade. It was granted Grade II* listing in 2007 and today the estate is better managed by the Byker Trust.

Opposite
Byker Wall, photographed shortly after completion

The Longfields

James and Jenny have been renting a three-bedroom house on the Byker estate for just over three years and have recently had a daughter, Beth. James is currently working on a PhD focusing on the Byker redevelopment and wife Jenny is a musician.

What made you choose to live in Byker?

[James] It was mainly my idea to move here. Having heard and read so much about it during my time at university I was really interested to know what it was actually like to live here, so we moved in as I was starting my PhD, though not knowing to what extent it would feature in my studies. Then it kind of took over! Even though we are only renting, moving here was seen as a bit of a risk as Byker has a bad reputation in Newcastle. It took a good year or so for the reality – that it is actually quite a calm and sociable place to live – to override these early concerns. It also helps that it is a lot cheaper to live here than elsewhere in Newcastle, it is really close to the city centre, and just a five-minute walk to the quayside on the Tyne with the Millennium bridge, Baltic gallery and Sage concert hall.

Describe your home

Most people associate Byker with the Wall, a mile-long perimeter block of flats which runs up the hill, but in behind the Wall the majority of the houses are low-rise, laid out in an irregular pattern around courtyards and green spaces. We live in a three-bedroom house in a short terrace with a shared grassy area out front, and a small garden at the back. It is a compact house, arranged around a central staircase, but has plenty of space for two and a small one.

What did you know about the estate before you moved here?

I knew a fair bit about the history, but neither of us knew much about what life was like in Byker beyond its reputation. We had some friends who lived here in the 1990s who told us stories of kids shoving fireworks through letterboxes and the like! I was initially a bit idealistic and Jenny somewhat uncertain, but we have found a happy medium during our time here. It definitely feels more and more like home.

Are the communal areas well maintained?

There are loads of varied green spaces with benches, planters and even quirky stone features, such as columns and carved reliefs, which were salvaged from the Town Hall in the city centre when they demolished it in the late 1960s. Originally there was a wide variety of planting as well as play features in these spaces, but these were ripped out in the 1990s. The council do a basic job of maintaining these spaces, cutting back hedges and mowing the grass a few times a year. Now the estate is Grade II* listed it is finally getting some much needed investment.

What are the neighbours like?

Friendly for the most part. We had one nightmare chap who lived next to us, but he has since moved and now there is a really lovely family next door. They gave us loads of great baby stuff just after they had moved in! We know most of our neighbours, and have kept in touch with a few who have moved out since we arrived. There is a real mix of people, locals who have lived here for years, a growing African community and more young arty types as we are right next door to a growing creative quarter. We like that people are very open and real.

What are the best things about living here?

It is wonderfully warm in the winter, the house has a great southern aspect, and is heated from a district heating system which we pay a flat rate for. It is also really quiet at night as there are no cars driving past, which is very pleasant. There are lots of blossom trees which are absolutely beautiful during the spring time.

What are the worst things about living here?

Our neighbour's kitchen window looks directly into our garden. Even though we enjoy chatting to him there are times when we want to enjoy some peace and you never know when he is going to pop his head out to say 'hi'.

If money were no object, where would you live?

We'd like to build a house one day, no idea where yet. Jenny would like to be somewhere with a bit more privacy, where she can play and record without being overheard.

Above
View into the dining area and stairs
from the front door

Above
Exterior view of the houses on Gordon Road

Above left
The master bedroom

Above right
View from the second bedroom

Opposite
Exterior view of Shipley Walk

Lillington Gardens

Pimlico London

Architects Darbourne and Darke

Lillington Gardens, built between 1964 and 1972, saw a radical departure from the Corbusian approach to mass housing that had dominated Britain in the 1950s and 60s. It was designed by Darbourne and Darke, the result of an open competition launched by the council in 1960. John Darbourne (1935–1991) won the competition and formed a partnership with Geoffrey Darke (1929–2011). The area had been earmarked for redevelopment in 1955 in the London County Redevelopment plan and the estate replaced streets of run down Victorian houses. Pimlico already had a reputation for high quality award-winning council housing with its Churchill Gardens Estate, designed by Powell and Moya in 1946.

The competition brief specified provision for schools, doctors' surgeries, playgrounds, pubs, shops, homes for the elderly, high-density housing as well as the retention of the Grade I listed Church of St James the Less, with its striking Victorian red brick. The final scheme comprises blocks ranging from three- to eight-storeys that have staggered facades with projecting bay windows and balconies adding individuality and character. It was the first medium-rise high-density estate in Britain.

Key to its success is the use of materials. It is sympathetic to its surroundings, particularly the church. The reinforced concrete buildings are faced with handmade red-brown bricks. The layout and design of the buildings have a sense of informality about them, but the use of brick gives them a more traditional feel. The scheme was built in three phases over eight years. The first phase was of particularly high quality as it was given additional funding so it could be built to a high standard and used as an example. All three phases are distinct in style, but the use of common materials unifies the scheme as a whole.

Particularly outstanding are the series of interlinking communal spaces, gardens and courtyards. The spaces vary in size and function and the landscaping is rich and green. Brick paved pedestrianised walkways are also landscaped and the overarching feeling is that of tranquility and privacy in the middle of London. Internally, many of the flats use split level scissor plans to maximise the space and light with either a large balcony, terrace or garden.

Lillington Gardens is much admired. In 1972 *The Times* described it as an 'elegant and exciting environment for young and old' and its concept was imitated throughout the country. It received four awards: the Housing Design Award (1961), Ministry of Housing and Local Government Award for Good Design (1970), RIBA Award (1970) and RIBA Commendation (1973). Today it remains popular and has not suffered some of the social problems of other estates. Phases one and two are Grade II* listed and phase three Grade II. It's worth noting, however, that Darbourne and Darke designed a similar scheme in Islington, and despite also winning awards its intricate layout made it impossible to police, and frightening for residents. It gained such a poor reputation for crime and vandalism that much of it was demolished and remodelled. Lillington Garden's proximity to Westmister and its high percentage of transfer to the private sector through the Right to Buy scheme has made it a much sought after estate.

Opposite
Lillington Gardens, photographed in 1972

Nicola Barton

As the daughter of an architect, Nicola grew up with an appreciation for buildings. She has lived in houses of varying styles over the years, but this is her first experience of living in a modernist property. She moved to her two-bedroom maisonette in Forsyth House, one of the first blocks to be built in Lillington Gardens, a year ago.

Describe your home
It's an upside down two-bedroom maisonette staggered over three half-floors. The bedrooms, kitchen and living room are all on different levels but the half flight of stairs between each floor make them feel connected. Originally the middle floor had a reasonably large kitchen and a little single third bedroom, but there was no room in the flat for a proper dining table so I knocked down the wall between the two rooms to make one big, bright room. There are large windows down one side of this room which makes it beautifully light.

The sitting room is at the top of the flat which spans the depth of the building and has a large window at each end. One of them looks out over the communal gardens at the back which is great, and the other looks out on to my roof terrace. The terrace is totally private with views of the Shard, the top of the London Eye and Westminster Abbey, and the big tower at Vauxhall.

The soundproofing in the flat is excellent. I very rarely hear any noise from neighbours. And being on a quiet street there is no traffic noise, so it is a very peaceful place to live which is amazing considering how close to central London we are here.

Did you know much about Lillington Gardens before you moved here?
I knew the area and had always admired this estate although I didn't really know anything about it until I mentioned to my father that I was thinking of buying a place here. Being an architect, he knew all about it as it won lots of awards around the time it was built. It is very cleverly designed so that each apartment has its own outside space and lots of privacy as there are very few places where you are overlooked.

Is the estate well looked after?
The communal areas are maintained by CityWest, who are the landlords, and they seem to do a good job. The gardens are nicely planted with mature trees, lawns and natural long grass areas. The covered walkways on each floor of the buildings have lovely wide raised beds that are planted with huge red geraniums.

What's the area like?
Pimlico is like a village. Tachbrook Street Market is just up the road which is excellent. It has a great fishmonger and butcher on Thursday, Friday and Saturday, there's a fruit and veg stall every day and lots of fast food stalls which are very good. There's a good range of shops close by which cover all the basics, from hardware shops to florists, bakers and supermarkets, and lots of cafes, restaurants and pubs. The locals are very friendly and having a dog means I've got to know people a lot more quickly than I would have done otherwise. It's a very mixed area which I like.

What are the neighbours like?
All very friendly, welcoming and neighbourly. There's quite a mixture of age, race and general background which is lovely. I think the best neighbourhoods are those with a mixture of different types of people.

What is the best thing about living here?
You have the best of all worlds – it's like living in a quiet village yet within easy walking distance from all the main parts of central London and several large parks.

And the worst?
I'm struggling to think of anything negative about living here! I suppose the worst thing for me is that I'm living in a flat which is leasehold rather than freehold, so I have no control over the running costs.

If money were no object, where would you live?
I would stay here and buy the flat next door, knock them into one and create a larger sitting room. I'd have a couple of extra bedrooms and a double sized roof terrace. But then that would be plain greedy!

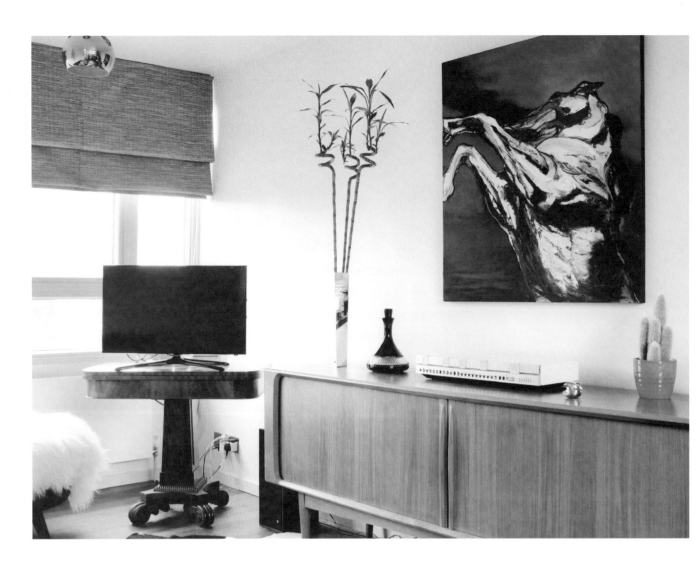

Above
The living room

Above
The living room, beneath the window would originally
have been a serving hatch to the kitchen below

Above left
The dining area, originally a third bedroom

Above right
The master bedroom

Above left
Looking down from the terrace

Above right
Exterior view of the estate

Christchurch Estate

Victoria Park London

Architects John Spence and Partners

The Crown Estate extends throughout Britain and comprises urban and rural estates, ancient forests, farms, parkland and coastline. It has significant holdings in London, most famously Regent Street, with a mixture of offices, homes, shops, restaurants, historic buildings, hotels and traditional clubs. Until recently it also owned four housing estates in London in Regent's Park, Millbank, Lee Green and Victoria Park, built as affordable rented homes to enable people working in essential public services to live near to their work. Their duty was to maintain and enhance the value of the estate and its revenue, but with due regard to the requirements of good management. Not having the budget restraints of local councils, the Crown Estate Commissioners were able to provide rented housing that was above the standard of local authorities. The Christchurch Estate near Victoria Park is a case in point. Designed by John Spence and Partners in 1967–77 it is built on a site previously occupied by a church on land owned by the Crown Estate. It comprises 149 low-rise dwellings – a mix of flats in three- to five-storey blocks, two-storey mews houses and four-storey blocks to the north that act as a barrier to the busy main road. Dwelling sizes vary and range from one person flats to family houses.

The estate was built in three phases: the first was completed in 1971 which included St Agnes Close; the second was completed in 1974 (Pennethorne Close, Vicar's Close and The Mews); the third phase in 1977 (Christchurch Square). The scheme was designed with sensitivity to the surrounding Victorian houses and successfully echoes the Victorian street pattern. The buildings are made from plum coloured brick, with simple windows in timber frames and aluminium covered roofs. The mews houses are a modern take on the traditional terraced house, with split level interiors, skylights and integrated garages and patios. Particularly successful is the landscaping and segregation of cars. The estate is divided into a series of courtyards with brick retaining walls containing grass, shrubs, exotic plants and trees.

Sadly, the Crown Estate sold off the Christchurch Estate, along with the three other London estates, to the Peabody Trust in 2011. They claimed they did not have the explicit expertise in managing social housing or the economies of scale from which larger housing associations benefit. This is yet another example of how the needs of people and communities have become secondary to financial profit making. The estate has fared very well today, which is testament to the Crown Estate as a landlord who successfully provided residential accommodation for nearly half a century.

Opposite
View of the first phase to be completed at St Agnes Close

Kirsty Carter, Arvid and Arne Niklasson

Arvid is originally from Gothenburg, Kirsty is English and grew up in Newmarket near Cambridge and they live in a two-bedroom mews house with their one-year-old son Arne.

Did you know much about the estate before you moved here?
[Kirsty] I remembered years ago getting lost cycling trying to find what is now referred to as Victoria Park Village. I thought I was taking a short cut and discovered the beautifully landscaped communal garden of Christchurch Square. I knew straight away this was a housing project that had been carefully thought through by a talented architect. I tried to find out more about it through RIBA and the Twentieth Century Society but didn't find out much. I certainly wasn't in a position to buy a house at that time, so I moved on and forgot about it.

Is the estate well managed?
There is quite a history with the management of the estate – it is now managed by Peabody, which provide provisions to key workers. When it was owned by the Crown Estate all the houses and flats were under leasehold to the Crown. When they sold it to Peabody the residents had the opportunity to buy the freehold of their house or block. We live in a block of six terraced mews houses and the way they are means you can't simply slice the houses into six. Four of us decided to club together and buy freehold of the block and manage it – we have one Peabody tenant and a leasehold tenant, so we are very much in charge of our own block. There is always this debate about painting the garages, front doors and gates a different colour, but the entire estate was painted blue by the Crown and was stipulated in their lease as cobalt blue to everyone. We can change this now but I don't think anyone can quite yet bring themselves to do it.

The estate has lots of communal areas which are beautifully kept. There are two gardeners that are in charge of the upkeep of the gardens, but they also act as the caretakers and keep the estate looking beautiful. Sadly due to the change of management, the estate is only just catching up with itself – things have been left to disrepair and are looking a little shabby. There are some major works due to happen this year, so that's very exciting. The cost will likely be covered by a sinking fund which has been built up. The estate is carefully gated just enough to keep children safe playing on all the paths, garden and roads. It feels a very nice place to bring up children – you don't have to keep an eye on them all the time and they can go on adventures with neighbouring friends. The children of the estate are always writing in chalk on the floor. I remembered when we just moved in someone had written in chalk, 'you are about to enter the best place in the world'.

What are the neighbours like?
We are very close to our neighbours, mainly because we own a business together, Pennethorne Close Ltd. We have directors' meetings to discuss the administration of the block. The neighbourhood overall is full of young families, architects and still lots of key workers.

What are the best things about living here?
We are right on the edge of Victoria Park where Arne can run and play. You can walk out of your door through the communal garden of the estate, right into the gate entrance of Victoria Park, which is just incredible! The house itself is very well thought through, open and light. The architects were just brilliant – even our north facing garden is in sunlight most of the day because the house is so low with no other houses interrupting.

What are the worst things about living here?
This is our dream home, but it is just a little bit too small. The bedrooms are very small compared with the living space. Arne's room is tiny and I can't quite imagine him being a teenager in there, so at some point we have to move, but I know very begrudgingly. We will have to keep an eye out for the larger houses on the estate coming up for sale, but they hardly do and it has become very expensive now.

Finally, with money no object, where would you live?
So many … but I'd say the Eames House, Case Study House #8 by Charles and Ray Eames in Los Angeles.

Opposite and above left
The living room

Above right
View from the kitchen up to the living room

Above left
The master bedroom on the first floor

Above right
The second bedroom on the ground floor

Above left
The bathroom

Above right
Exterior view

Dunboyne Road Estate

Gospel Oak London

Architect Neave Brown

Between 1964 and 1978 Neave Brown (b. 1929) worked on three housing projects in North London: a group of five houses at Winscombe Street, a housing scheme at Fleet Road (Dunboyne Road Estate) and his largest scheme Alexandra and Ainsworth Estate, all of which are now listed (Grade II with the exception of Alexandra Road which is Grade II*) making him the only living architect to have all of his UK work listed.

Born to an American mother and British father, Brown spent the majority of his childhood in the US before coming to London to study at the Architecture Association in London after the Second World War. Here he found himself with like-minded liberals such as John Miller, David Gray, George Finch and Patrick Hodgkinson. The post-war reconstruction programme offered Brown and his contemporaries an opportunity to build a new, more equal society and to try to dissolve the distinction between public and private housing. After leaving the Architecture Association, Brown worked for a number of private practices including Lyons Israel Ellis, as well as teaching. In the early 1960s with the ambition to design his own house for his young family, he joined forces with a group of friends to form a housing co-operative. They persuaded Camden Borough Council to lend them the money to buy a neglected pocket of land in Dartmouth Park to build five homes. These five identical houses became a prototype for Brown's later schemes – the division of the space with the 'adult zone' on the top floor, the children's bedrooms on the ground floor with access to a communal garden, and the kitchen and dining areas in the middle are themes and ideas repeated at both Fleet Road and Alexandra Road.

Sydney Cook, Camden Borough's architect from 1965–73, was so impressed with Brown's houses that he offered him a position to join their architecture team and gave him his first major commission – a housing project on a site in Gospel Oak. The area had previously been home to run-down Victorian houses. The planners, wanting to achieve the highest density possible, had ear-marked the site for redevelopment with typical high-rise blocks. By this time, Brown and some of his contemporaries had become sceptical of the ordinary mixed and high-rise developments that were being built across London. Tall buildings were proving impractical for families and the visual landscape of London was beginning to change. Before the war the majority of housing consisted of rows of terraced housing, stepped back from the street a few feet, with a private garden at the back serviced by an alley. In the Fleet Road scheme, Brown reinvents the traditional London terrace, preserving its scale and intimacy. There are a total of seventy-one units of maisonettes and flats, in two- and three-storey blocks which run in parallel rows with a central pedestrian walkway (the alley) providing access to the front doors of the lower flats. A mix of one, two and three bedroom dwellings are arranged cleverly to maximise light and flexibility of space. Each has a private terrace and its own front door, shared gardens while car parking is integrated below.

The construction of the Fleet Road scheme took much longer than anticipated due to a number of complications, but was finally completed in 1977. It became the first high-density low-rise scheme to be granted planning consent and to be built. It exceeded the expectations of the planners by achieving an even higher level of density than their strict person-per-acre quotas, and is an important prototype of modern housing built in a pattern that conforms to a tradition and culture of the English terraced house. Along with his other schemes, Dunboyne Road Estate has established Neave Brown as one of the greatest housing architects of his age.

Opposite
View of the roof terraces and balconies, photographed in 1978

Neave Brown

Neave and his wife Janet share their time between their two-bedroom house in Dunboyne Road Estate (Fleet Road) and their second home in France. Since retiring from architecture he has concentrated on practicing fine art.

Briefly describe your home
It's a two-bedroom, four-person ordinary council house, built to council house space and budgets – but with different thinking.

How long have you lived here?
About six years. We lived at Winscombe Street previously – my first housing scheme to be built, having originally moved there with a group of our contemporaries: architects, a photographer, a painter. We loved it. We all had children, there was a communal garden which the children adored, it was a wonderful place to live. Then inevitably people changed, some people moved away and new people moved in. And my wife and I began to feel like the 'special geriatrics' that had been left there. It's a place for young people and young families.

What made you decide to move here?
I asked Janet, my wife, where else she might like to live, and she said she had always liked Fleet Road. At the time I was in touch with somebody who lived here, so I rang her and asked if there was anything going and she said yes, the house next door was on the market. I went to the estate agents straight away and put an offer in.

Did you have any concerns about moving from a house to a council estate?
No! Because my generation are post-war people. After the war I studied at the Architecture Association and our teachers were mainly young modernist architects. London was in ruins. There had been lots of planning, but very little rebuilding. All the young architects were taking what they had learnt in the interwar years – Le Corbusier, the Bauhaus etc., and brought that new architecture to a new age and new culture to England but rejecting the tabula rasa of that Modernism.

We would help build a new and mixed society – eliminating the old class system. Unfortunately many of us feel disappointed, the triumph of capitalism has betrayed the egalitarian ideals that we had.

What are the neighbours like?
There are still people here that moved in when it was first built, and the children of those first residents too. We say good morning to everyone. The person next door is a very good friend. That's the way it should be. But of course, this scheme – like every other scheme – has been betrayed by Margaret Thatcher's Right to Buy policy. But then again it's a mixed society, which was always our intention with professionals and, to use that terrible term, working class people. You get an additional pleasure out of the mix and that's nice. I hope it's that way at Alexandra Road, it was at Winscombe Street.

What are the best things about living here?
Who am I to say, but it's beautiful. It's spacious, we get lovely light, we have the marvellous terrace where Janet and I sit and have breakfast and supper, the front doors connect straight on to the street so that you feel you belong to the city and are not separate from it. The plans are such that you get an incredible amount of flexibility with the space.

What's the worst thing?
The worst thing is what has been imposed by the government – they have betrayed the idea of housing that was set up after the Second World War, and the social intentions that went with it. Affordable housing should mean it is affordable for a good lifestyle for people on minimum or low income – which is what was done when we did it. Housing was literally affordable for people on working class incomes, and if they couldn't afford that there were other subsidies that were available in government programmes, so that people on very low incomes could live decently.

If money were no object, where would you live?
Here!

Above
The kitchen and dining area

152

Above
View up to the living space from the kitchen

Above
The living space, with patio doors to the balcony

Above left and right
Glazing above the stairs to maximize light

Above left
The master bedroom

Above right
Second bedroom, both bedrooms have
access to a terrace

Opposite
Exterior view of the estate

Alexandra and Ainsworth Estate

Swiss Cottage London

Architect Neave Brown

In 1967, before the Dunboyne Road Estate was even completed, Sydney Cook commissioned Neave Brown to design Camden's most impressive and striking social housing project – the Alexandra and Ainsworth Estate. With its huge continuous sweep of terraces divided by pedestrian walkways, the estate is instantly recognisable. It has been used as a backdrop to numerous films and television shows and has been likened to the Royal Crescents of Bath with concrete overcoats.

The housing brief for the 16 acre site was initially fairly typical, but grew to become quite elaborate. Brown was asked to include, alongside homes for 1,660 people: a tenants' hall, underground parking, shops, workshops for Camden's Building Department, a school for children with learning difficulties, a children's reception centre, residential accommodation for young physically handicapped people, car parking and a public open space, as well as integrating the existing neighbouring Ainsworth Estate.

As in his previous schemes, Brown opted for high-density low-rise blocks and here the street is ever more prominent. The blocks run east to west, with a seven-storey stepped block running along the edge of the Euston Mainline railway (forming an acoustic barrier) and opposite a four-storey block, both overlooking a terracotta paved street. To the south is a further terrace block which consists of three-storey houses separated by a landscaped three-acre park.

Each of the 520 dwellings is given either a large terrace or garden, and internally the spaces feel light and generous with sliding partitions making them flexible and spacious despite being designed to council housing size standards. Central heating was ingeniously buried into the walls which allowed for more space for furniture. The care devoted to the internal fittings was perhaps unique among local authority departments at the time. Each has its own front door with a direct connection to the street. The public green space forms an integral part of the overall architectural scheme and is intersected by walls of white board-marked concrete, forming a highly structured series of outdoor 'rooms' with built-in concrete seating. Car parking is integrated below, along with a gas boiler house.

The estate was given Grade II* listing in 1993, but ironically this would be the last project Neave Brown would design in the UK. Construction costs of the estate began to soar as inflation rose in the 1970s, a new housing director at Camden was fiercely opposed to the scheme and tried to stop it being built. Concerned that they would never be able to justify the expensive housing for working class people, the council tried to distance themselves from it. Ken Livingstone, who became chair of Camden's Housing Committee in 1978, was also against the scheme and set up a public enquiry to investigate 'what went wrong' with Alexandra Road before it was even finished. The enquiry saw the end of Brown's career in the UK.

Brown fought hard to ensure the scheme would be completed and succeeded. The first residents finally moved in in 1978. Despite what Camden thought, people did want to live there, and today it is home to a strong and mixed community. Maintenance of the estate has been notoriously bad and neglectful however, and the once crisp white concrete is now stained and dirty. Once again the optimism of the architects and their belief that their buildings and tenants would be well looked after has fallen foul of the local councils who commissioned them. The majority of the estate is still home to council tenants and the now celebrated project has become a mecca for architecture students and enthusiasts the world over.

Opposite
The central pedestrian walkway, photographed in 1979

Eleanor Fawcett, Nathan and Nina Jones

Eleanor and Nathan both studied at the University of Cambridge and MIT in the US. Nathan is now an architect and Eleanor heads up the design team at the London Legacy Development Corporation. They bought their house in Alexandra and Ainsworth Estate four years ago and have recently had their first daughter Nina.

Did you know much about the estate before you moved here?
We knew about the estate as an iconic Brutalist project. One of our close friends from architecture school wrote his dissertation on it, and then moved into a flat on the estate. Having said that, it wasn't really on our radar as a place for us to move to. But as soon as we came to see the house we were smitten – it was so much more spacious and light than anything else we'd seen – and much better value!

Are the communal areas well maintained?
The main pedestrian areas are fairly well looked after, but the park in the middle of the estate known as Alexandra Road Park has been neglected since it was finished in the late 1970s, and is in a pretty overgrown and sad state today. But it's a really unique modern landscape. Eleanor got involved in a project to apply for funding to restore it when we moved here, and it received over £1 million funding from the Heritage Lottery Fund. Works are now underway and will be finished this year!

What are the neighbours like?
Fantastic – it's a really friendly and diverse community. We've got to know loads of people from the estate since we moved here, which has been an unexpected bonus. This is partly because we've got involved in lots of activities – including the tenants' association, the park restoration project and a weekly fruit and veg co-op on the estate – but we also feel that the design of the estate is another reason why it's such a friendly place. The communal spaces are so integral to the design – and the way that everyone's terrace and front door connects directly to these spaces means that you can't help but feel connected to your neighbours. There was a lovely film 'One Below the Queen' made by residents about the

estate when we were thinking of moving here. It really captures how much people enjoy living here, and how proud they are of the bold architecture. There are lots of residents who moved in when it was first finished in 1979, and have stayed ever since – which gives you an idea of its success.

What are the best things about living here?
Getting involved with the community and, of course, the design of our house. Some of our favourite things about the house are:

The panoramic view of the trees from the full-width strip window in our kitchen – the view changes throughout the year, and feels like living in a park.

The way the staircase runs up through the centre of the open plan living spaces, making all the floors feel really connected.

The huge sliding doors, and generosity of the full height doorways.

The 'upside-down' arrangement, with the bedrooms on the ground floor and the living room at the top.

The big roof terrace, which connects to the living room and feels like a real outdoor room.

What are the worst things about living here?
Nothing really! But it's never ideal being at the mercy of Camden Council on service charges.

Finally, money no object, where would you live?
In a house we designed for ourselves, somewhere in central London!

Opposite
The dining area which is situated
on the second (middle) floor

Above left
Newly installed kitchen

Above right
View into the study, originally
a third bedroom

Above left
Staircase

Above right
The top floor living space

Above
View of the terrace on the
top floor of the house

Whittington Estate

Dartmouth Park London

Architect Peter Tábori

Camden Council, with Sydney Cook at the helm as chief architect, was proving to be the most progressive and exciting borough in London in the late sixties with a real commitment to good quality social housing. Cook employed the best young talent and developed a style now referred to as 'the Camden style': low-rise blocks, clean lines, narrow windows with dark wooden casements and large front windows. Sitting on the border of Highgate Cemetery in Dartmouth Park lies the Whittington Estate – rows of crisp white, angular ziggurat buildings with street-like pathways running between them. It was designed by the Hungarian architect Peter Tábori (b. 1942) who had previously worked for Denys Lasdun and Ernö Goldfinger. Having studied at the Regent Street Polytechnic it was suggested by his tutor that he go and see Cook with his student project to see whether there was a site available where it could be built and realised. Cook was immediately impressed with the young architect and employed him to design his scheme on part of a site (Highgate New Town Phase I) that had previously contained dilapidated hundred-year-old housing.

As in Neave Brown's Alexandra Road, the twenty-six-year-old Tábori was concerned with bringing the street into his design as the centre of community life. The low-rise concrete blocks are organised into long terraces with pedestrian walkways and play areas so that children can play outdoors, away from traffic, and still be overlooked by their parents. Despite the buildings being no more than two-and-a-half storeys high, a density of 200 bedspaces was achieved with a mixture of flats, maisonettes and houses. Each dwelling has a south-facing balcony and its own front entrance directly from the street. There's also a considerable amount of landscaping. At a time when car ownership was rising, Camden demanded that a huge amount of space be given to car parking, so Tábori revised his designs and substantial underground car parking was incorporated – which in later years had to be closed off due to the dark, hidden areas attracting crime.

Construction of the estate was meant to last only two years with completion scheduled for 1974, but blighted by a number of complications – not least the construction company going bust half way through the project – it took an extra five years and went four times over the original budget. The first residents moved in in 1979. Somewhat jaded by the experience, Tábori went on to do a couple of further schemes for Camden but none as successful as the Whittington. Today the estate is well looked after and home to a mixed community and is especially popular with architects and designers, with a high percentage of flats being transferred into private hands having been bought through the Right to Buy scheme.

Opposite
The children's play area on the Whittington Estate, photographed in 1979

167

Andrew Rae and Chrissie MacDonald

Illustrators Chrissie and Andrew met in 1995 while studying at Brighton University and co-founded the illustration collective Peepshow, with a group of their contemporaries. They run a studio in east London although since moving to the Whittington Estate a couple of years ago, Andrew generally prefers to work from home.

Tell us a little bit about your home
We live in a four-bed house over three floors, with the entrance on the middle/raised ground floor along with the kitchen and one bedroom/study. The other bedrooms are on the floor below and an open plan living space on the top which clinched it for us as it's such a great open space with fantastic light and a balcony.

Did you know much about the Whittington Estate before you moved here?
We lived in a one-bed conversion down the road for a few years so we knew we loved the area and from

walking past so often had grown more and more fond of the estate. We immediately fell in love with the house for its modernist aesthetic and attention to detail in the design, like the shadow gaps around the doors and windows and floor-to-ceiling doors, plus the amount of space you get for your money is a lot more than you would get in a Victorian house for example. Having lived in a conversion it's great to live in a home that's purpose built with a well thought out floor plan. Plus the previous owner had already done a great job doing the place up which meant we just needed to give it a lick of paint.

Is the estate well maintained?
The exterior of the buildings were painted a few years ago so they look good. All the communal areas are outdoors and are well kept, especially the greenery throughout the estate which we pay for through our service charges (which includes the heating and hot water that runs from the communal system, repairs and daily rubbish removal).

What are the neighbours like?

We've met lots of great people through residents' meetings and from walking around the estate, some who have lived here since it was built, like our neighbour next door, and others who have moved in more recently. It's a real mixed bag but we've never met so many architects! The estate was built with the intention to house tenants from a broad range of society, which is definitely the case and as it's pedestrianised the kids all play outside together without fear of the traffic. It's easy to bump into neighbours and have a quick chat or wave from the balconies, there's a real sense of community.

What are the best things about living here?

It's really peaceful in our home as it's so light and airy and you can see a lot of sky from the balcony. There's Waterlow Park and Hampstead Heath along with lots of great pubs and cafes nearby. Archway and Gospel Oak stations are close by and you get the great mix of being positioned between high-end Highgate – where you can go for an overpriced coffee and see how the other half live – and eclectic Archway and Holloway Road full of loads of handy shops and Turkish cafes.

And the worst things?

Having to deal with Camden Council as the freeholder can be frustrating, although they do seem to be trying to engage with the residents recently so at least there's a process that you can choose to be involved in.

Finally, what's your dream home?

If we were to stay in the UK we are where we want to be, but would love to live in the Eames Case Study House #8 for a year or two please.

Above
Exterior view of Sandstone Place

Opposite
View of the stairs from the ground floor

Above
The living space on the top floor which
spans the full depth of the house

Above
The dining area in the kitchen

Opposite
The terrace

London Borough of Lambeth

Architect Edward Hollamby

Whilst Sydney Cook, as borough architect for Camden, was gaining a reputation for progressive low-rise, high-density housing in North London, Edward Hollamby (1921–1999) at Lambeth Council was at the forefront of a similar, yet quieter, revolution in South London. He worked his way up the ranks at London County Council in the 1950s and 60s, working on notable projects such as the Brandon Estate in Kennington and the Pepys Estate in Deptford. As the LCC disbanded he was offered the job as Chief Architect at Lambeth in 1963 and later became their Chief Planner.

Although not against tall buildings per se, Hollamby did believe they should only be built if the site warranted it, and he led a campaign to encourage low-rise, high-density building. This, along with the Ronan Point disaster of 1968, would see the decline of high-rise building. Hollamby was a strong believer in conservation and would seek to retain and bring up to standard good quality old buildings on sites, integrating them with new developments. Lambeth Council was inspiring and progressive at this time and Hollamby employed a team of some 750 staff. With supportive, like-minded and progressive government ministers Hollamby was responsible for a great number of good quality, small, mainly infill schemes for the borough including May Tree Walk, Cressingham Gardens, Myatts Field and Central Hill Estate, and won a number of awards. Surprisingly, the most progressive of the schemes were built under a Conservative government.

Hollamby sat in the opposite camp to many of his contemporaries who were influenced by Le Corbusier. He believed people did not want to be housed in large estates, no matter how imaginative the design and convenient the dwellings, and preferred more humane designs, which were modern yet retained a continuity of tradition. He was also a great believer in listening and responding to the communities for whom he was building. In the scheme at Central Hill in South Norwood, for example, there was much opposition to building the new development so Hollamby suggested he would meet the local residents in a pub to go through the plans with them. This proved very successful and he won support and backing for the scheme.

Having little time to design buildings himself, he divided projects between six or seven groups, each with its own personality and leader. He would brief the teams at the start of a project with his own particular view on it, including specifics such as maximum height and his preferences regarding materials. He would ensure the ethos of Lambeth would be carried through into every development – to create delightful, exciting but not overwhelming, liveable housing relating to their surroundings. The estates were almost always built from good quality materials such as slate and London stock brick, flats and houses built around courtyards with cars restricted to the perimeters. Careful landscaping, trees and buildings such as community centres were all important parts of the designs. Front doors often faced each other with kitchen widows facing the walkways to promote neighbourliness. Internally the dwellings were designed to maximise daylight with full height glazing and skylights. The results were successful communities in village-like, well-thought-out, humane estates.

Today, many of the Lambeth estates which have been subject to poor maintenance over the years, and are on prime land, are threatened with demolition and regeneration, including Cressingham Gardens. This process has faced public opposition, spearheaded by a strong-knit group of local residents. For Myatts Field North it is too late, a large part of the estate has already been demolished and the area, rebranded as the Oval Quarter, will offer 357 homes for private sale, 146 as shared ownership and 172 existing homes will be modernised and refurbished.

Opposite
May Tree Walk Estate, an example of Lambeth's patio housing, 1971

175

Ruth Lang

Ruth is an architect, lecturer, journalist and is currently doing a PHD on the LCC Architects' Department. She lives in a three-bedroom patio house in Myatts Field South in Brixton, built in the mid-1970s under Edward Hollamby with Bill Jacoby as the chief architect.

Did you know anything about Myatts Field South before you moved here?
I knew absolutely nothing, but I was drawn in instantly. I knew there was something special about this place – it's been really well thought out in terms of how people use it, not just in the layout of the estate, but the spaces in the houses too. All the terraces have a private south-facing garden, as well as a little buffer space at the front which gives another layer of privacy from the communal areas. I fell in love with the way light is brought into the centre of the house by the split roof section – the bathroom is like a cathedral, it's a glorious space to lie in watching the sunset in summer, or with the rain lashing against the windows when it feels like the most protected space in the world. We thought the house was brick construction when I bought it – the council only found out that they're all timber framed when they tried to undertake insulation works earlier this year. I was lucky though – this place had been derelict for six years, and was cited in a question to Eric Pickles in parliament as one of the examples of council housing that they had no idea what to do with. It was sold for (relative) peanuts at auction after that, completely gutted and turned for a profit – it's sad to see the old auction photos of it in such a state with grilles over the windows, but if it hadn't been, I don't think I'd have ever been able to afford something like this.

Is the estate well looked after?
The council tend the gardens on a near daily basis and trim back the plants every couple of months. The council still provides district heating for most of the tenants, although they're forever trying to remove it. I'm hoping they don't succeed as it's all housed in a giant concrete submarine down the road, another brilliant quirk that shows what a sense of humour the architects had at the time.

What are the neighbours like?
Even as I was moving in everybody stopped to introduce themselves and to offer help. Coming from Shoreditch where I barely said good morning to my neighbours more than twice in four years, this was a bit of a shock at first. One of the nicest small design features is that the front doors open facing one of our neighbours, which means you bump into them for a chat quite a lot, and you know there's always someone there with half an eye on what's going on.

Best things about living here?
It's brilliantly located, ten minutes from Brixton, Stockwell or Oval, but as it's pedestrianised it's still incredibly quiet. It's got so much character, especially in comparison to the anodyne development of the Oval Quarter they're building to replace the other half of the estate at Myatts Fields North. The design definitely contributes to building a sense of community too – it feels like home, rather than just a place I live.

Worst thing about living here?
Being a contributing factor in the inevitable gentrification of the area irks at my conscience still. I know it's 'people like me' who are changing the area from what we know and love, and it's an awkward conundrum. I certainly couldn't afford to buy here now, and I have a constant, underlying concern for how that's going to alter the area in the long term, and what will happen to the people who are displaced.

Finally, money no object, where would you live?
I'd have to get back to you about this, the list is just too long …

Above
Exterior view of the estate

Above
The living room and patio garden

Above left
The landing which is lit by a skylight

Above right
The study, originally a third bedroom

Above left
The bathroom

Above right
The master bedroom

Greenwich Millennium Village

Greenwich London

Architect Ralph Erskine

As you arrive at North Greenwich tube station, part of the Jubilee line extension of the late 1990s, and head towards the colourful Greenwich Millennium Village with London Mayor Boris Johnson's cable car running across the Thames, you'd be excused for thinking there's something of the Noddy-town about the place. It is perhaps the most interesting and ambitious housing scheme to be realised in recent times, and only a twenty-minute journey from central London.

Built on a brownfield site, it was formerly home to the largest gas works in Europe and as a result was heavily polluted with over 120 hectares of toxic wasteland. At great expense the area was cleaned up and a masterplan drawn up by Ralph Erskine following an international competition launched by the then Deputy Prime Minister John Prescott in 1997. The competition sought to promote new thinking on how to achieve a sustainable urban development in the twenty-first century. Erskine, with his reputation for innovative ways of working, and architects Hunt Thompson Associates collaborated to design a model scheme that was both ecologically sensitive and sustainable – it boasts an 80 per cent reduction in primary energy consumption, 30 per cent reduction in water usage, 80 per cent recyclable building materials and zero CO_2 emissions.

Working with Taylor Woodrow and Countryside Properties the architects proposed a scheme for a 32-acre site which would contain 1,079 flats and 298 houses. Innovative ways of building were encouraged and industrialized methods were adopted, for example whole bathrooms including all the plumbing, were constructed off-site and slotted into the dwellings – making, in theory, the construction time 25 per cent shorter and therefore reducing the overall costs.

The first phase of the scheme consisted of 450 homes, an ecology park and artificial lake, all designed by Erskine, who was eighty-three at the time. A stepped building wraps around the lower rise buildings – similar to his Byker Wall – and provides shelter from the harsh east winds. A series of courtyards and pedestrianised areas provide a human quality and places to socialise. Erskine believed car usage would decline in the future and the use of the car here is actively discouraged. The whole area is designed with an emphasis on walking, cycling and the use of public transport, with cars banished to the perimeters of the estate. Mixed tenure housing was integrated, with no distinction between social and privately owned housing. A school, health centre, shops and commercial buildings were all part of the scheme. As in Byker, there a rich mix of materials, colours and textures – external walls are cladded with terracotta tiles and render, and roofs covered with aluminium. As much light was brought into the interiors as possible with floor-to-ceiling glazing, and living areas often open plan.

By 1999, however, disagreements between the developer, Erskine and Hunt Thompson Associates forced both architects to resign. They claimed their designs had been revised and compromised to such an extent that the developer had failed to deliver on the environmental credentials they promised. The second phase of the scheme was designed by Proctor and Matthews and sensitively developed a distinctive style to echo Erskine's initial phase. Today the building work continues generating an estimated total of 1,800 homes by the time it is completed. Now in its fifteenth year it will be interesting to see how the buildings fare with the test of time.

Opposite
Maurer Court, Renaissance
Walk, fronting the ecology park
in Greenwich Millennium Village

Paul and Susie Blackburn

Paul and Susie run a design studio just fifteen minutes' walk from their flat in the first phase in Greenwich Millennium Village. They share their penthouse home with their daughter Ava and miniature schnauzer Pixel.

How long have you lived here?
We have lived in the village for the past twelve years – this is the second property that we bought here. We originally lived next door in an apartment that we bought off-plan in 2002. Whilst living there we always had our eye on this one, and when it came on the market in 2008 we jumped at the chance to buy it.

What attracted you to living here?
The architecture really attracted us because at that time 'modern' residential architecture was a rarity in London. We'd read about the development, had an interest in the Scandinavian look and feel of the design and the ecological credentials of the build, and came down to have a look at the area. A couple of hours later we'd placed a holding deposit and retired to the local pub to calm our nerves. It was only after purchasing that we began to research the work of the architect Ralph Erskine. This obviously has deepened our understanding and appreciation of Greenwich Millennium Village.

Are the communal areas well maintained?
Yep; mopped, dusted and polished at all times. The communal courtyard gardens are an absolute joy. There is a village team of eight including a concierge who are great and on hand 24/7. The upkeep is good, a piece of litter or overgrown shrub doesn't stand a chance and there's a pro-active approach to maintaining the communal gardens. A sinking fund has been built up over the last few years and the development is about to get its first major spruce up.

What are the neighbours like?
All our neighbours are great and are a healthy mix of young families, city workers, pensioners, teens, creatives and thankfully the odd babysitter. We know many of them socially and frequently end up having a drink or two on someone else's balcony or terrace.

What's the area like?
The village has all the good, basic facilities we need: a small supermarket, dry cleaners, chemist, coffee shop, spa along with a bakery stall at the weekends for all your croissant requirements! There is a beautifully designed junior school and a local pub called The Pilot. It's a ten-minute walk through the Peninsula Park to the O2 which has attracted many conventional bars and restaurants as well as recently some more interesting independent ones, along with a new gallery.

The transport links are super good, a two-minute bus ride or ten-minute walk to North Greenwich tube station on the Jubilee Line from where it's a fifteen-minute tube journey to the West End. There are alternative modes of transport here too, the cable car across to Excel (should you ever wish to go there!) and the Thames Clipper which is a river boat service that travels as far as Westminster making many convenient stops along the way. The whole peninsula is served well by car-free cycle paths, and strict parking rules ensure that traffic is kept to a minimum.

What are the best things about living here?
The peace and quiet of being by the river yet still closely connected to central London. The modern architecture, the staggering views down the river to the Thames Barrier, especially at first light, the people and the wonderful ecology park.

And the worst?
It would be nice to have a butcher or fishmonger within walking distance, and of course the recession has slowed down the speed of the remainder of the development build, although that now seems to be picking up pace.

Finally, money no object, where would you live?
20 Blackheath Park, the house designed by Peter Moro – architecture porn heaven.

Above
View from the main living space
towards the dining area and kitchen

Opposite
The dining room

Opposite
The master bedroom

Above left
The bathroom 'pod' which was prefabricated
off-site and slotted into the apartment as one unit

Above right
The kitchen

Above
View of part of the the dining room from the kitchen

Above
Large private terrace